ADULT COLORING BOOK
MANDALA

Pure Relaxation & Stress Relieving Abstract Patterns

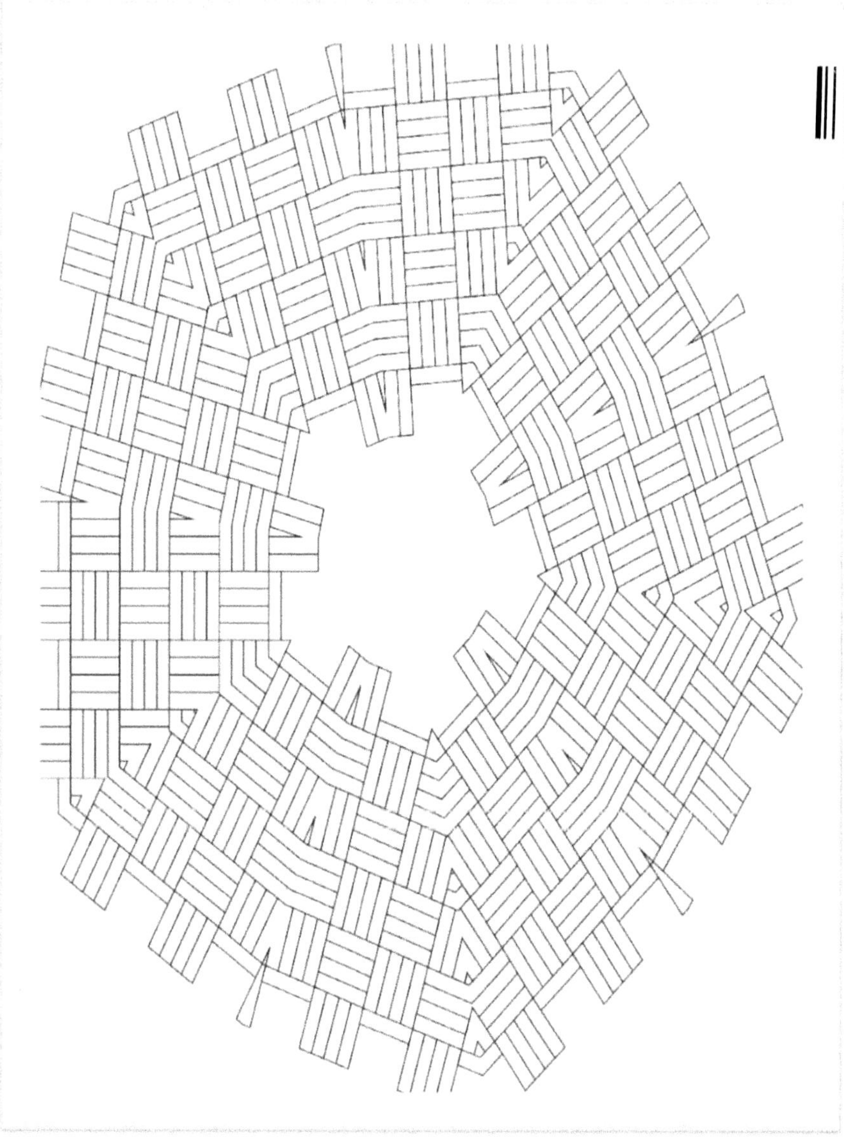

Over 40 Symmetrical Mandalas & Geometric Patterns

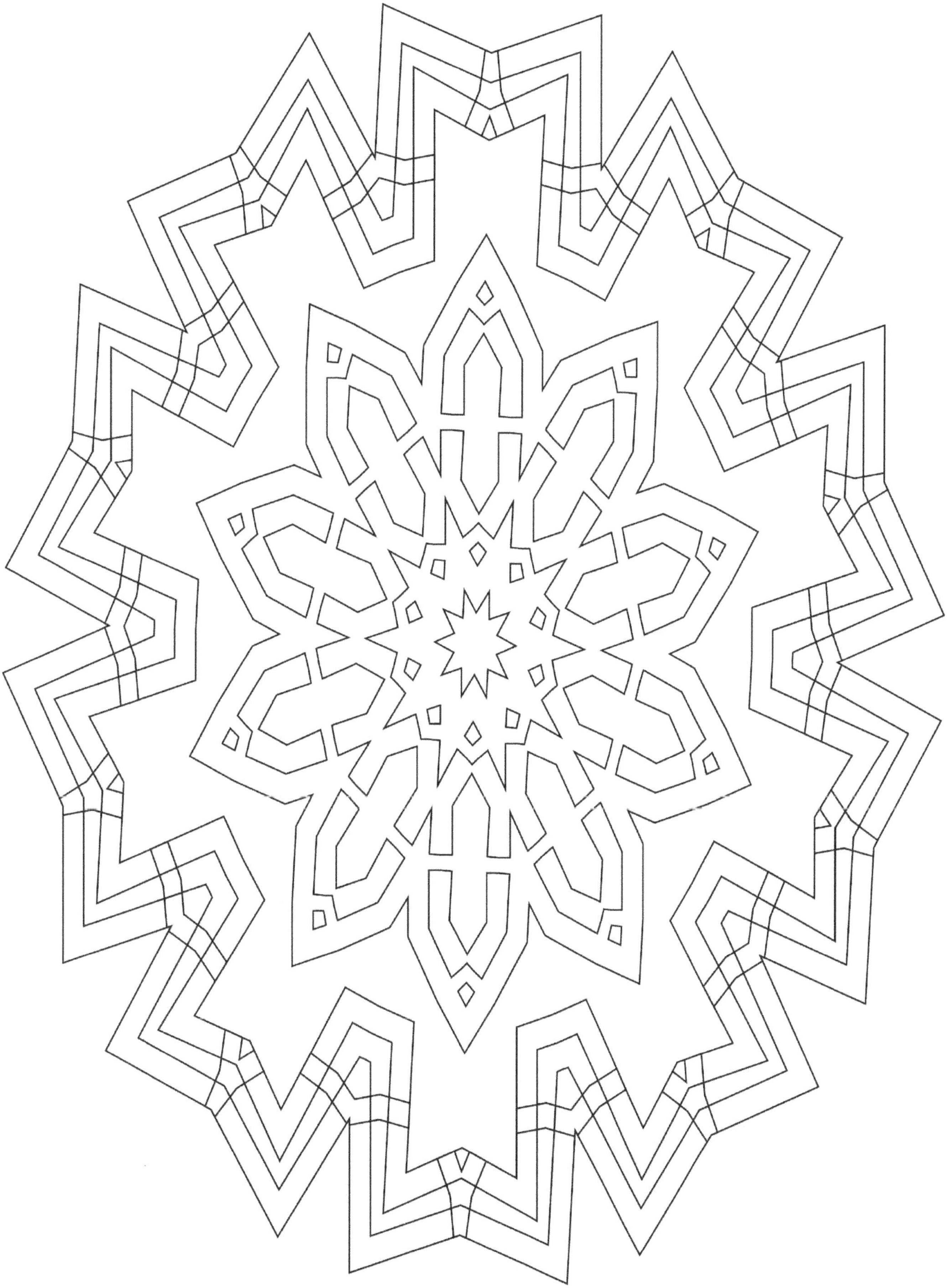

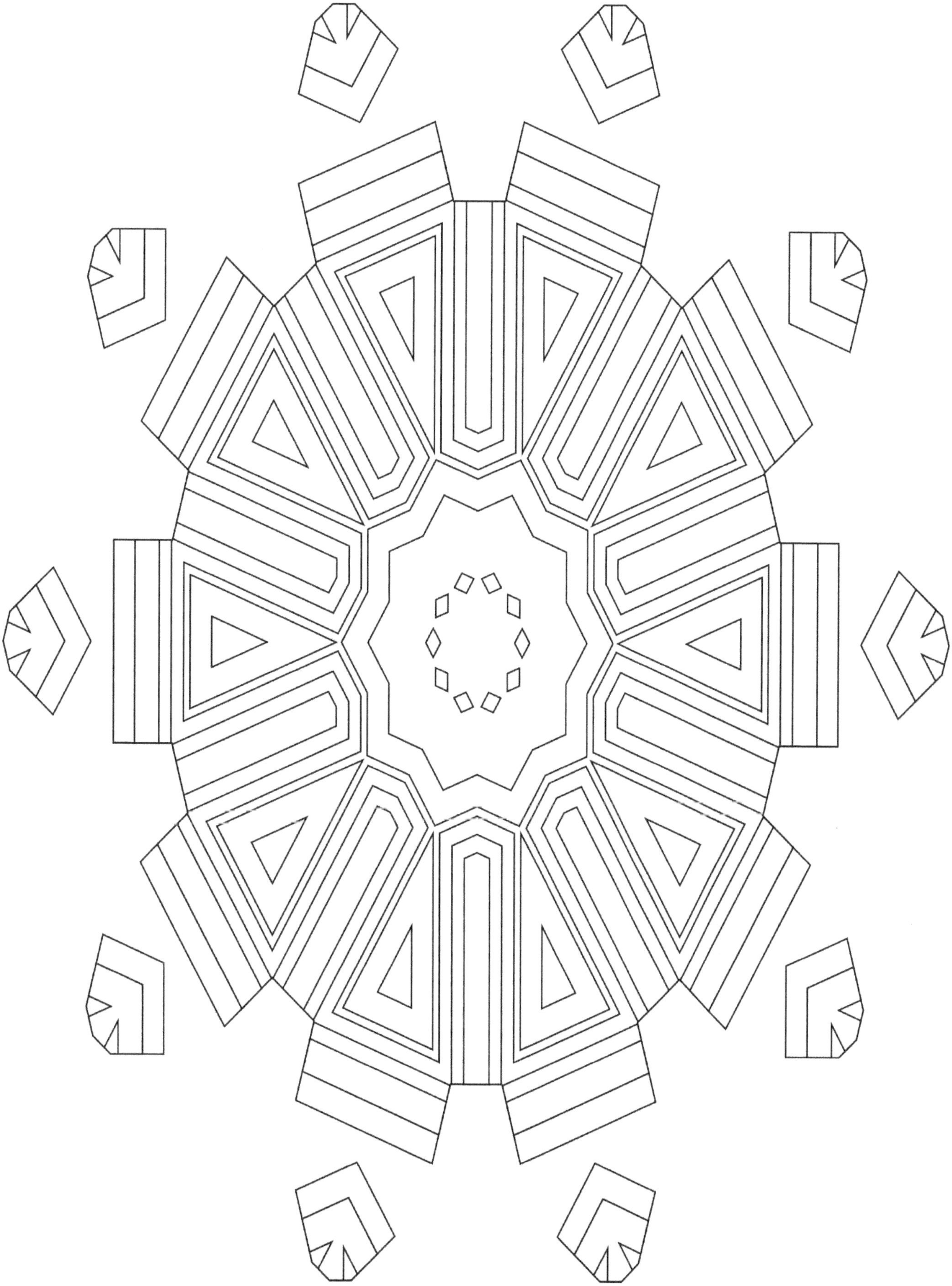

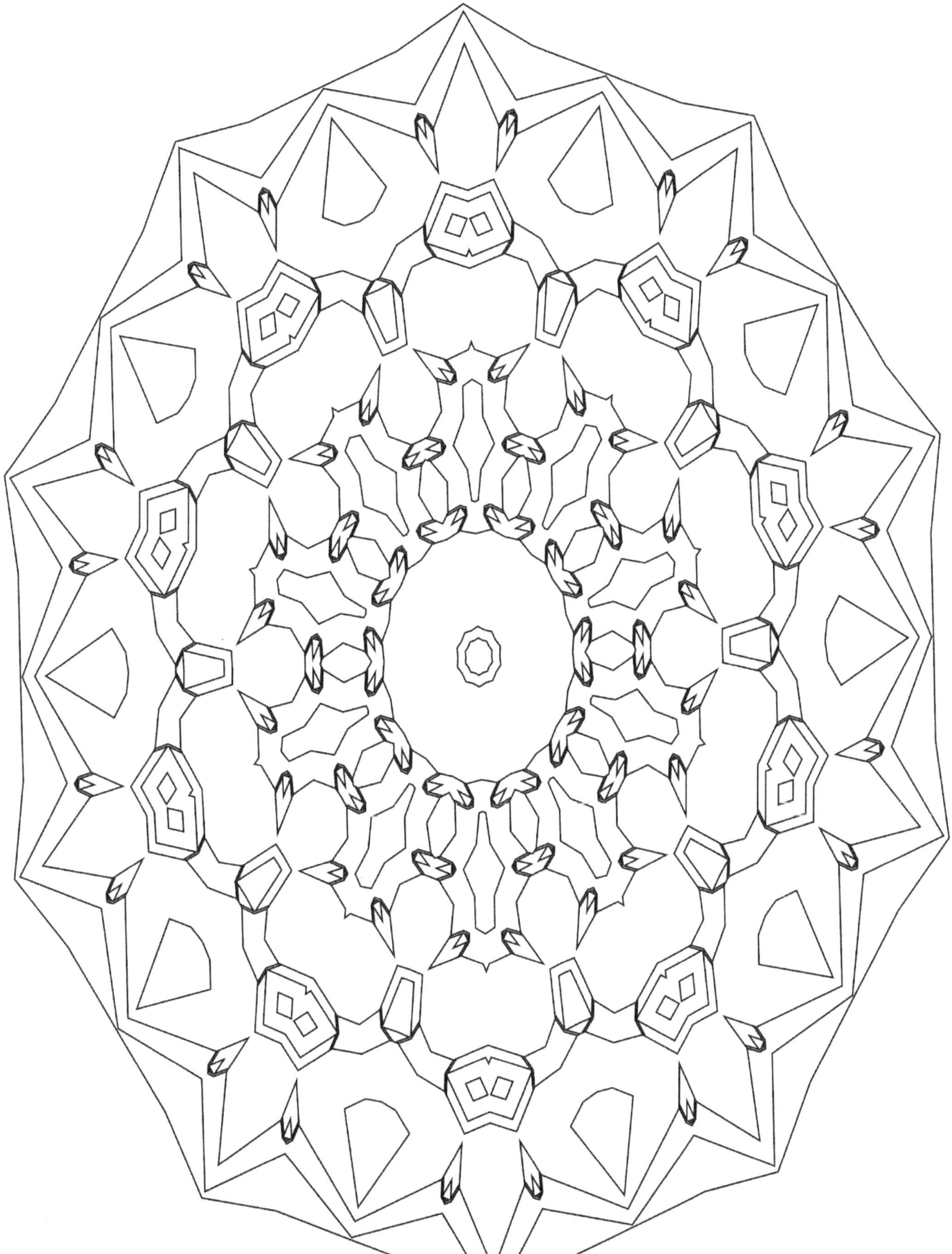

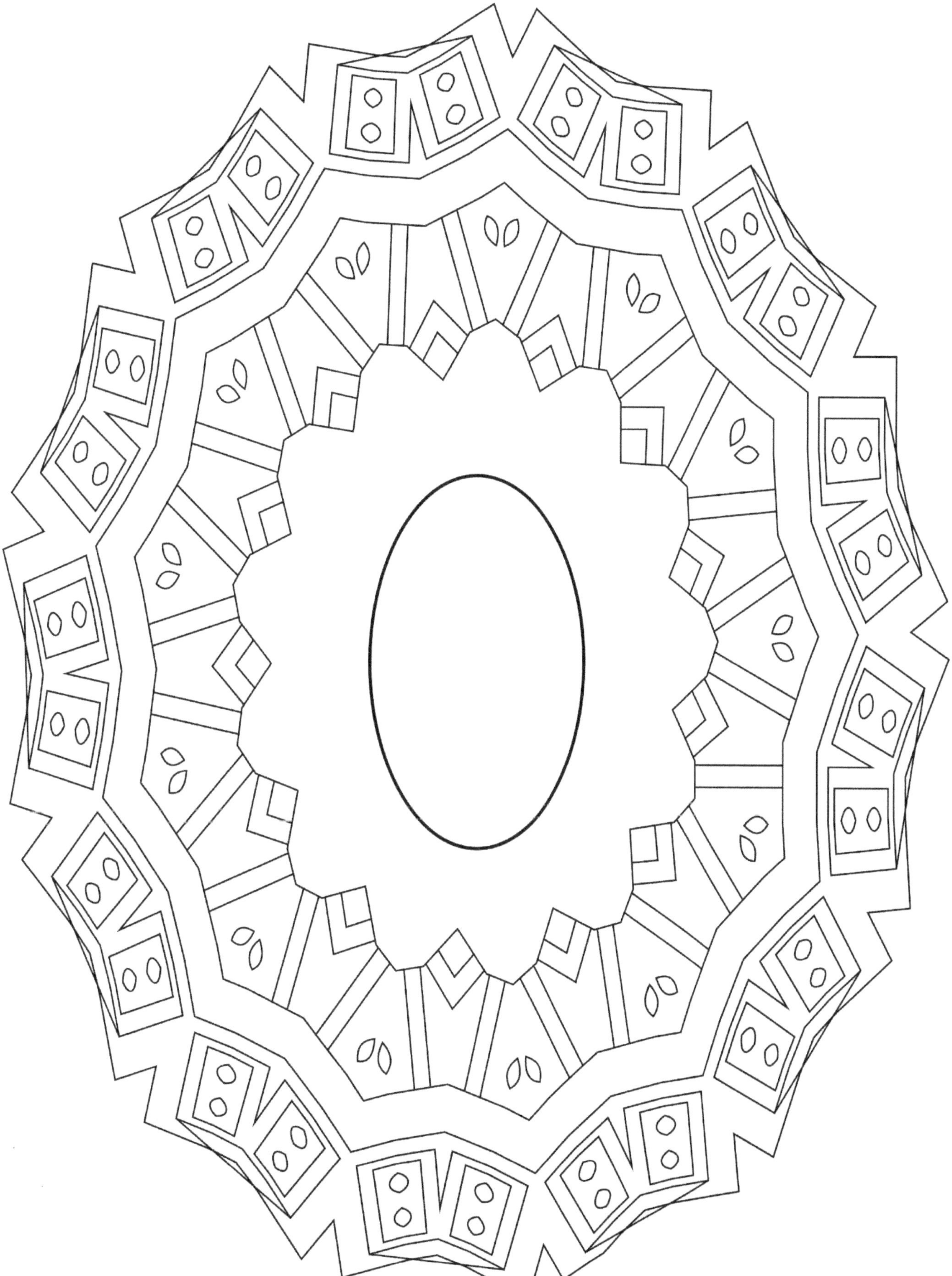

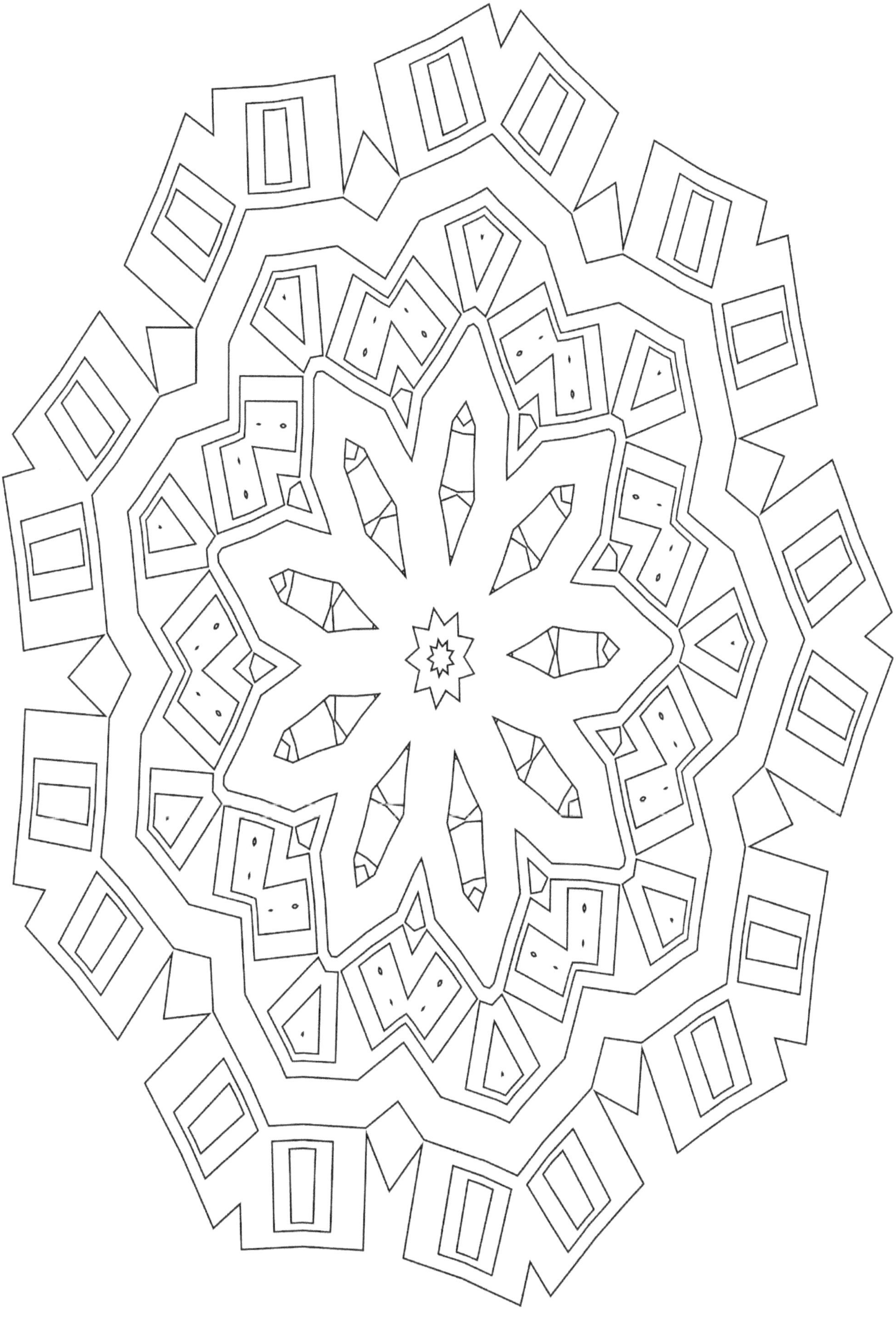

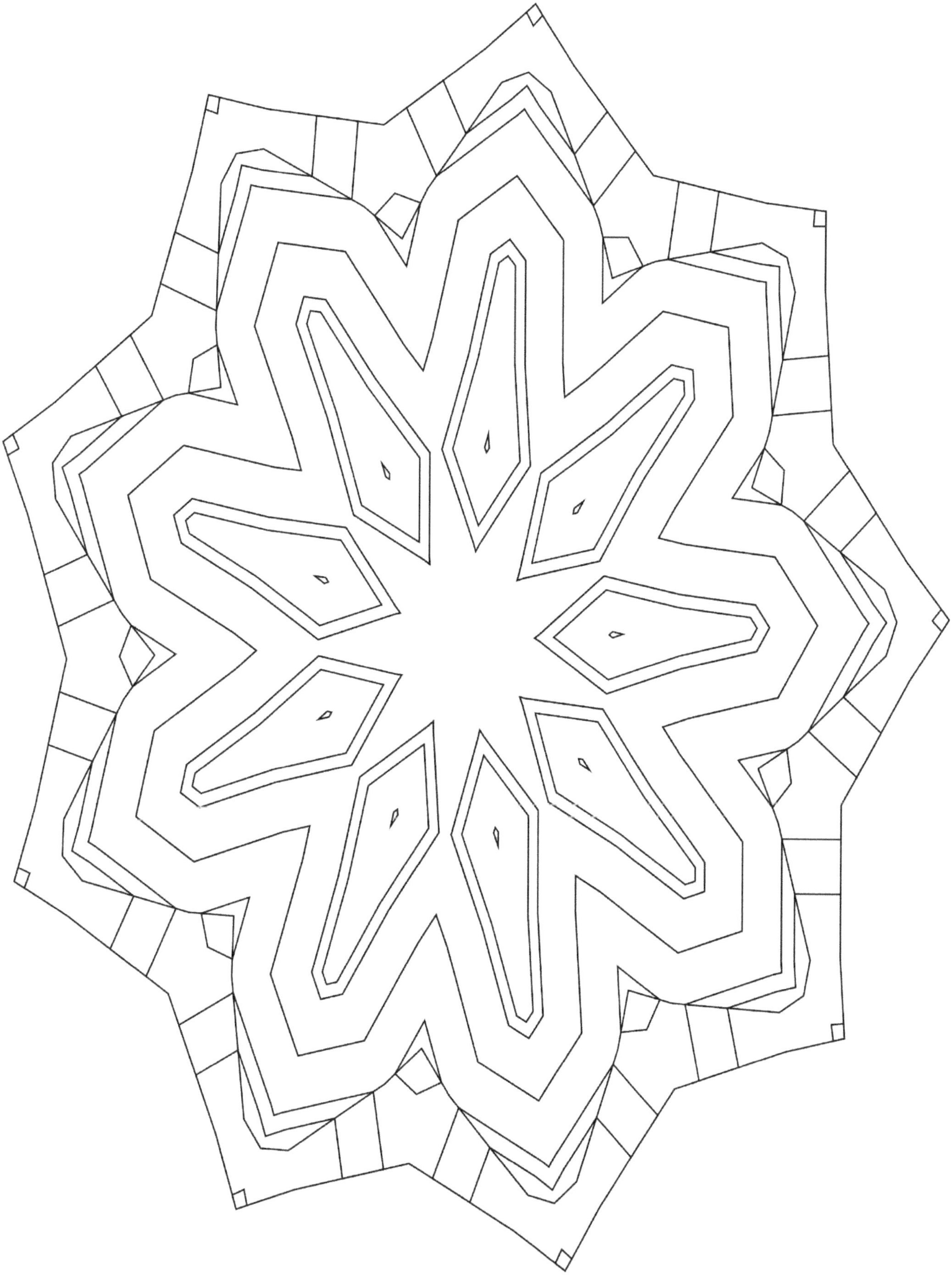

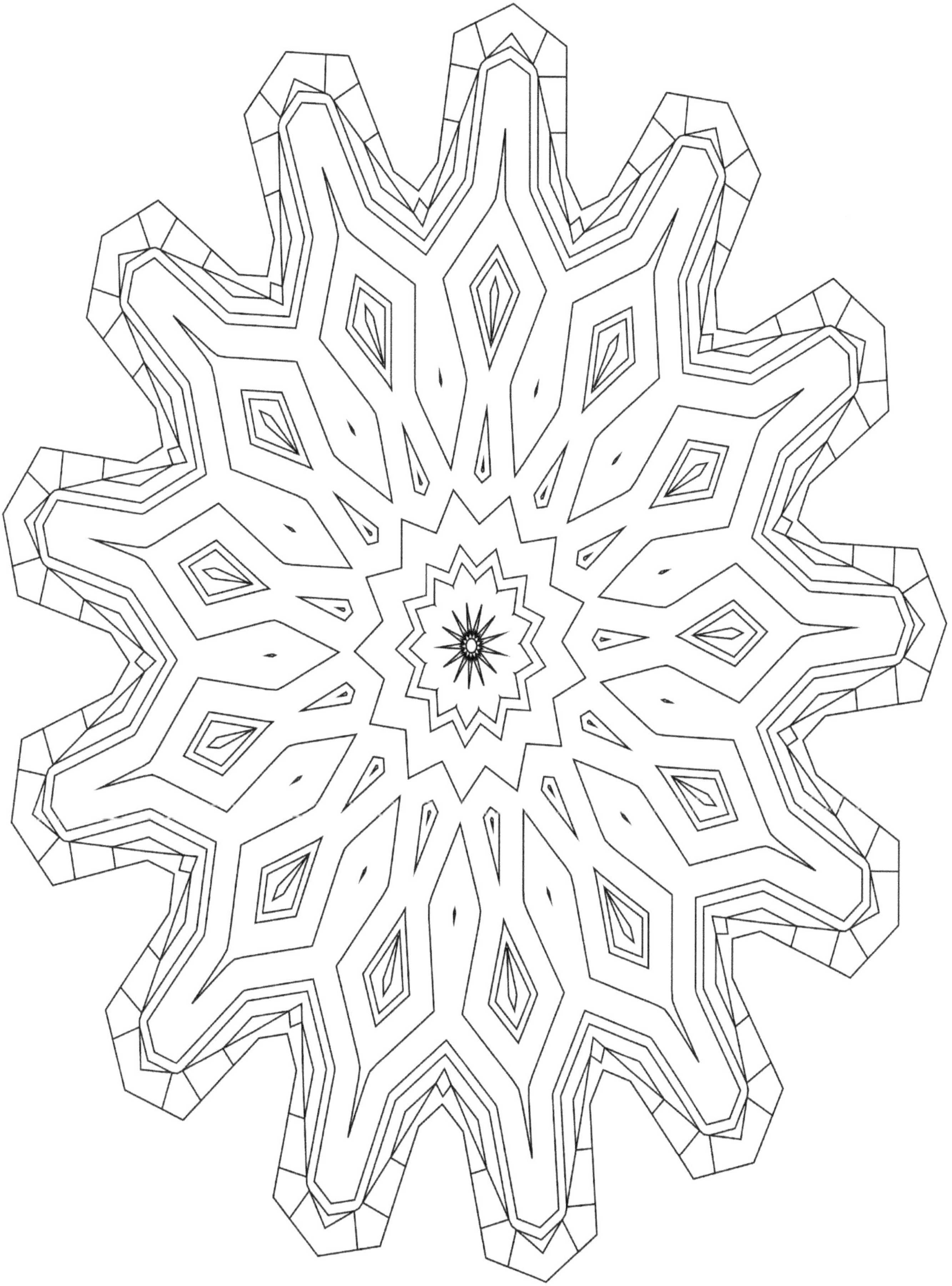

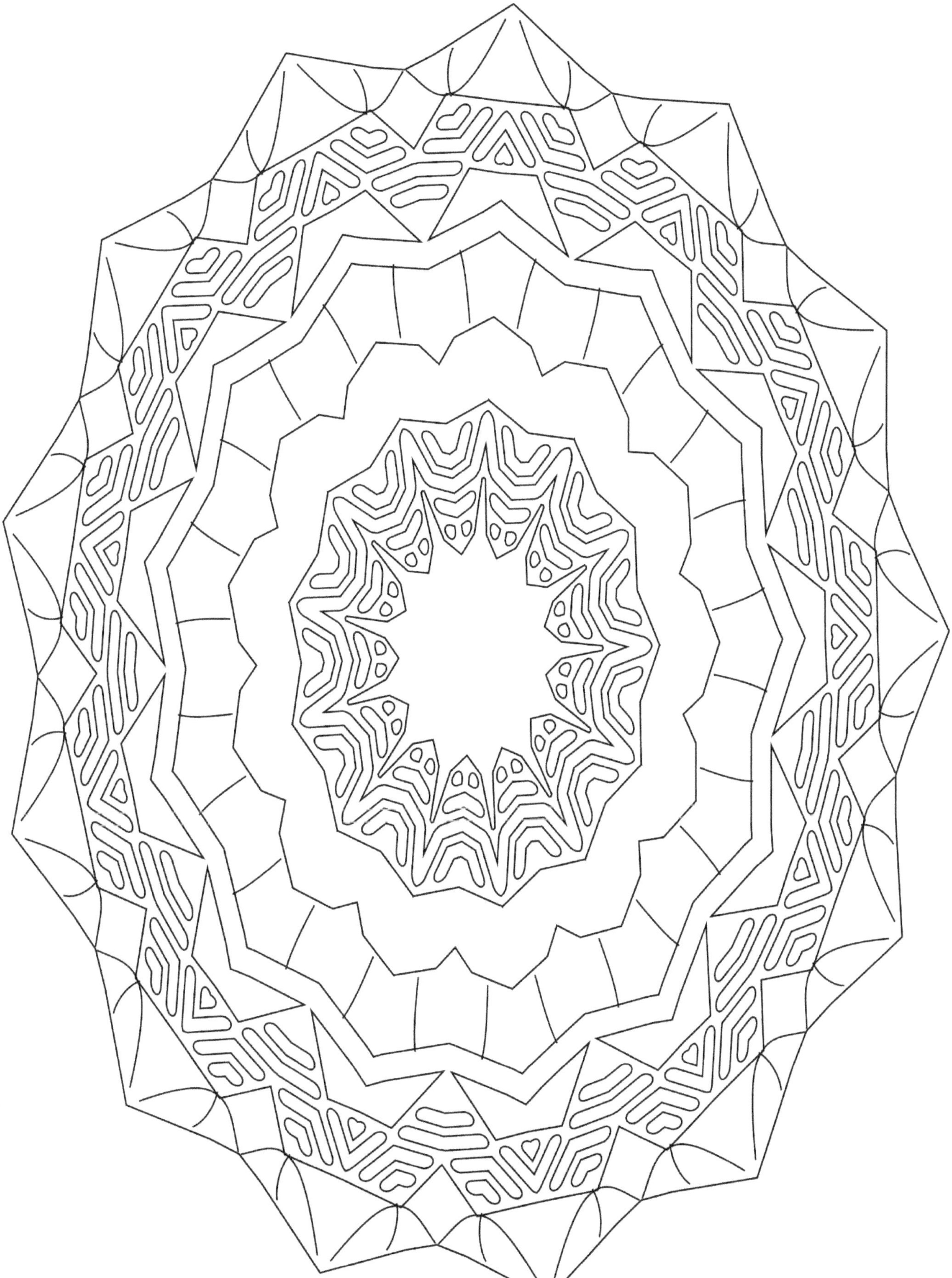

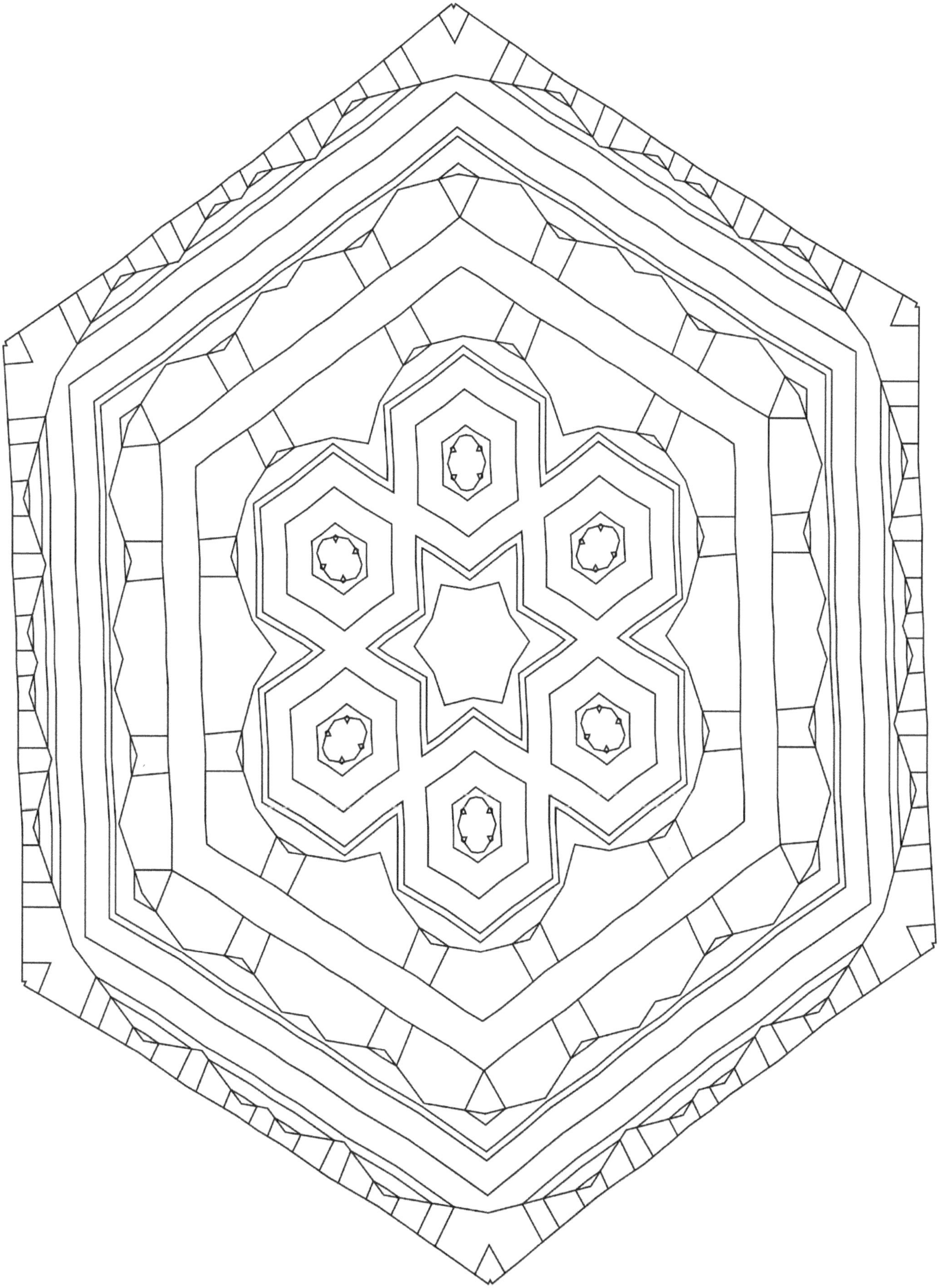

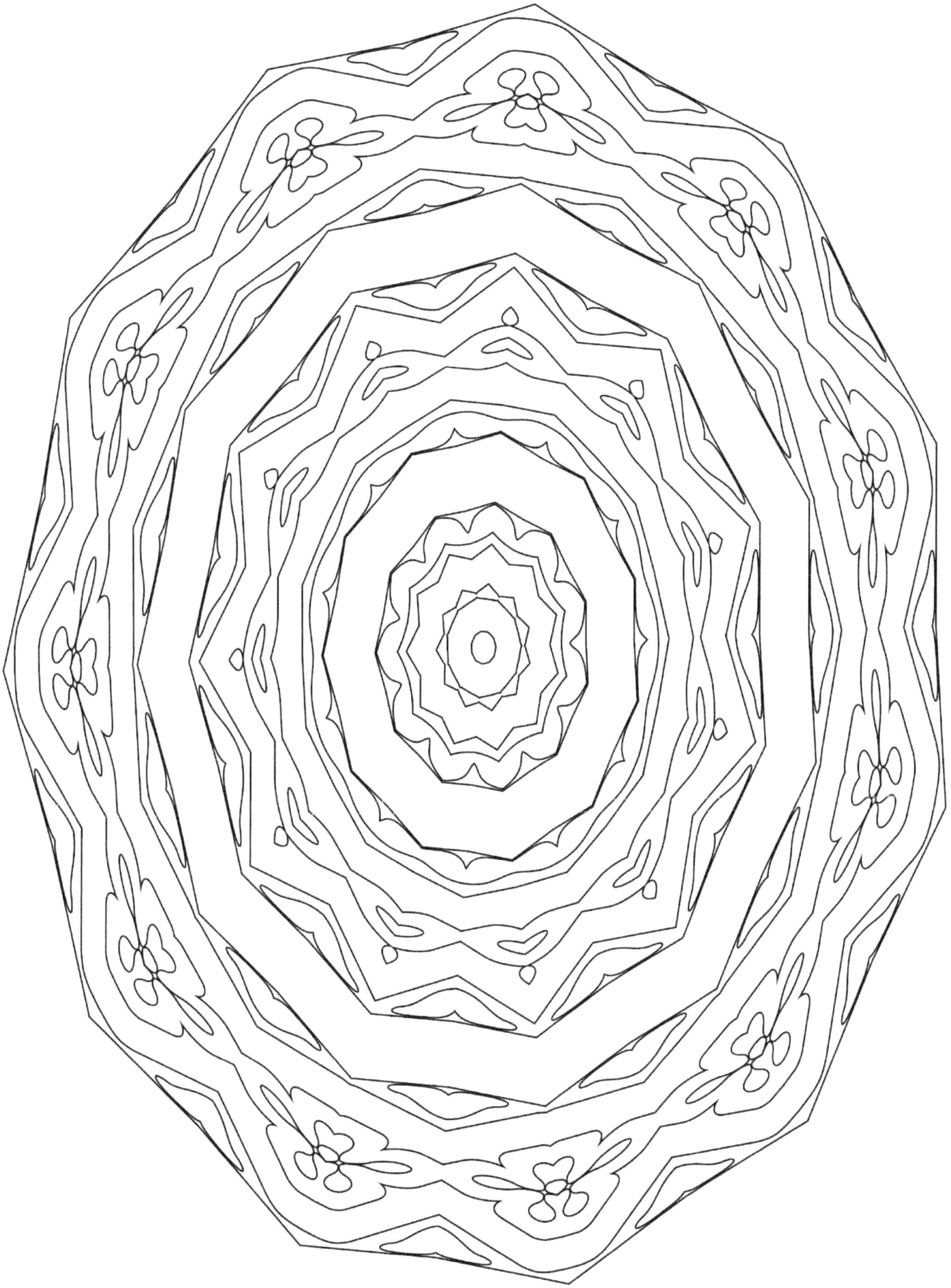

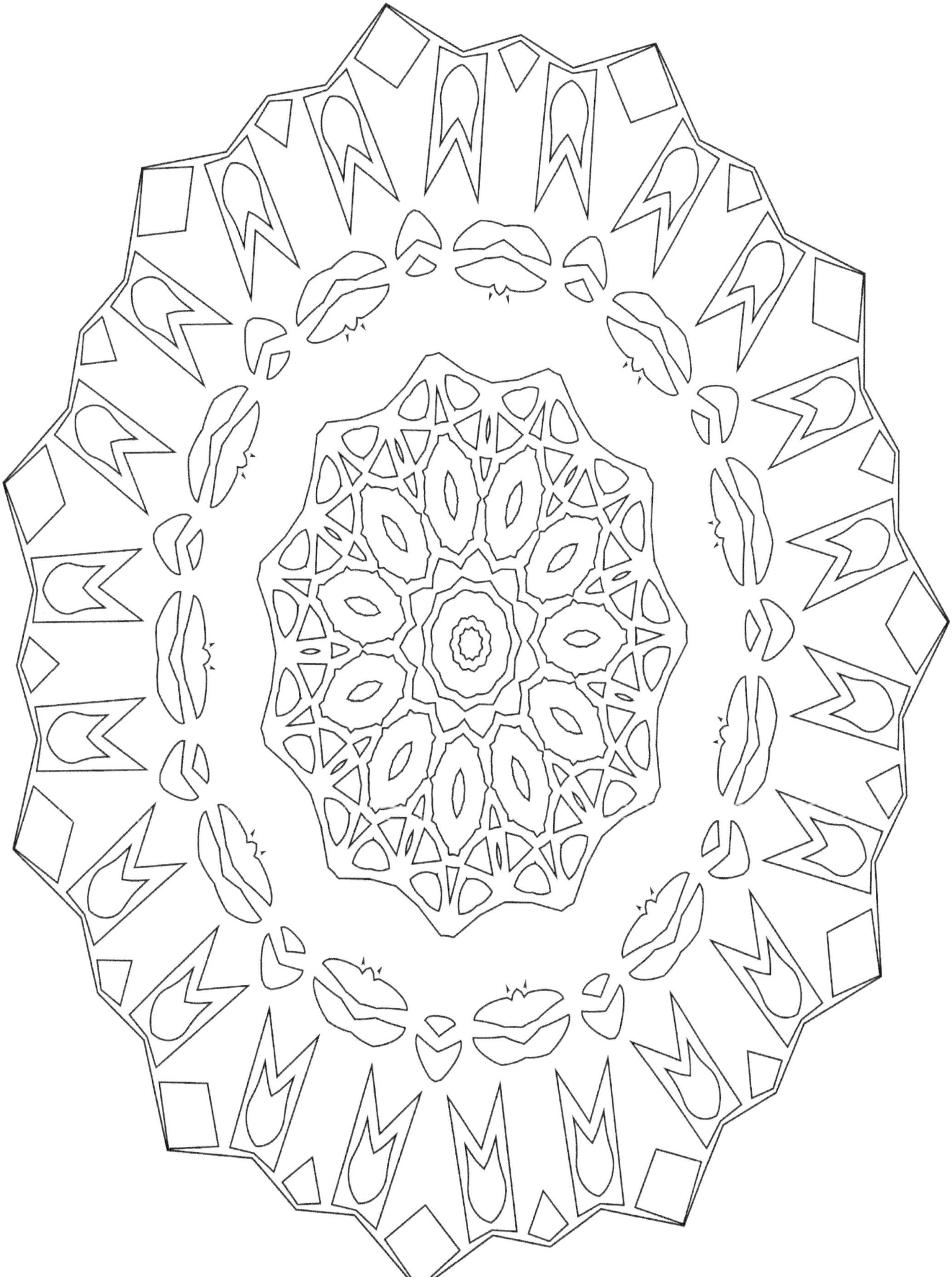

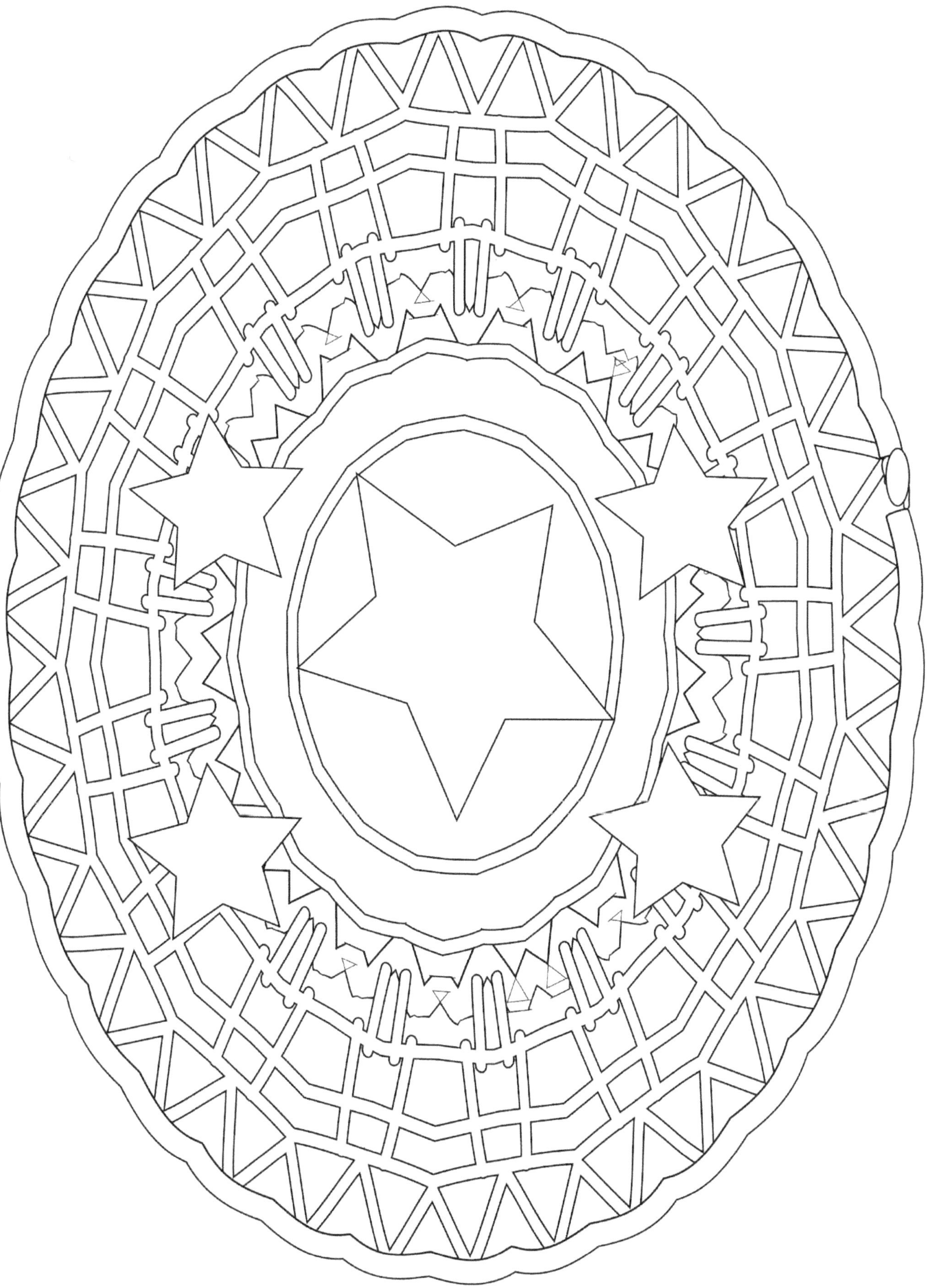

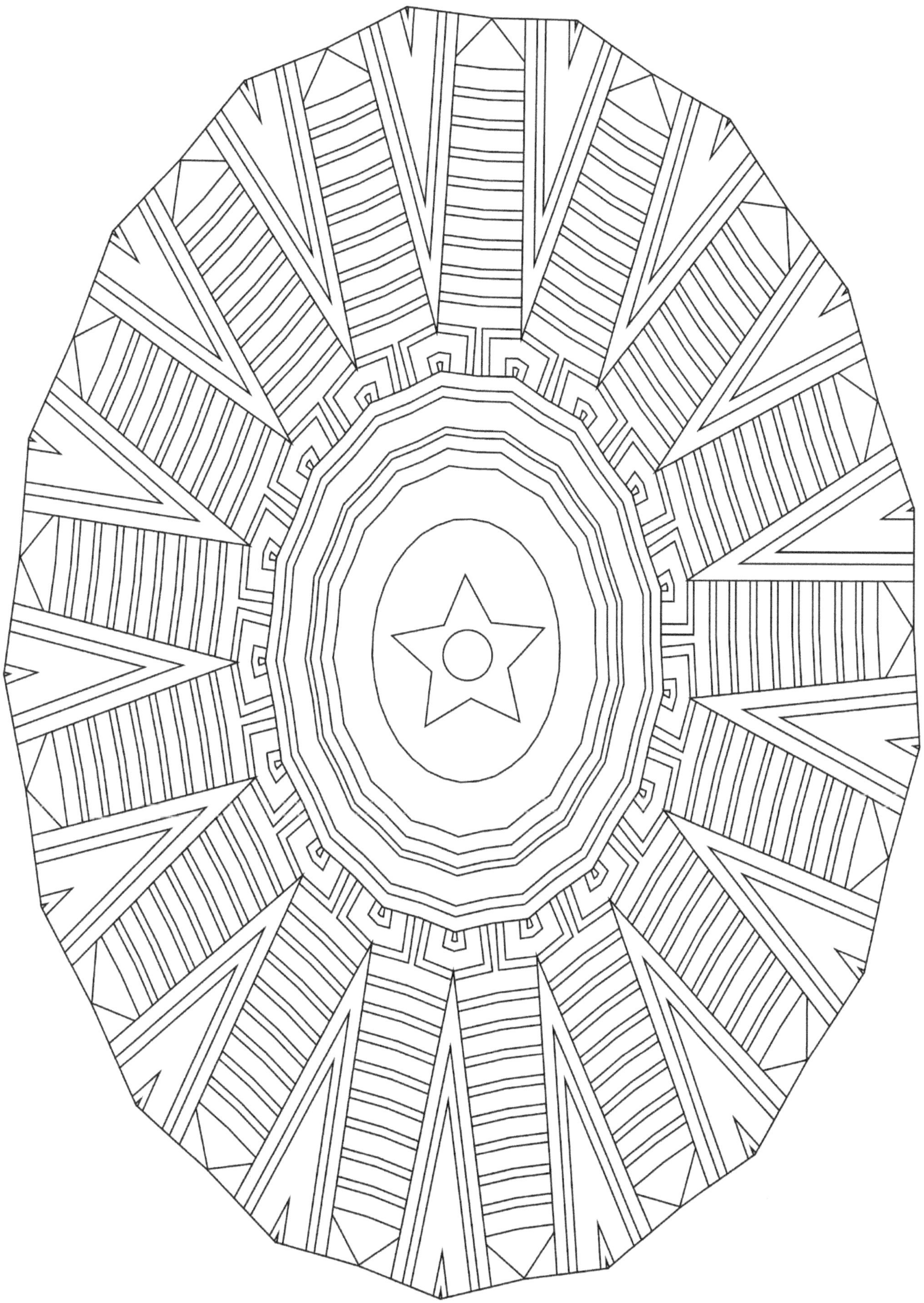

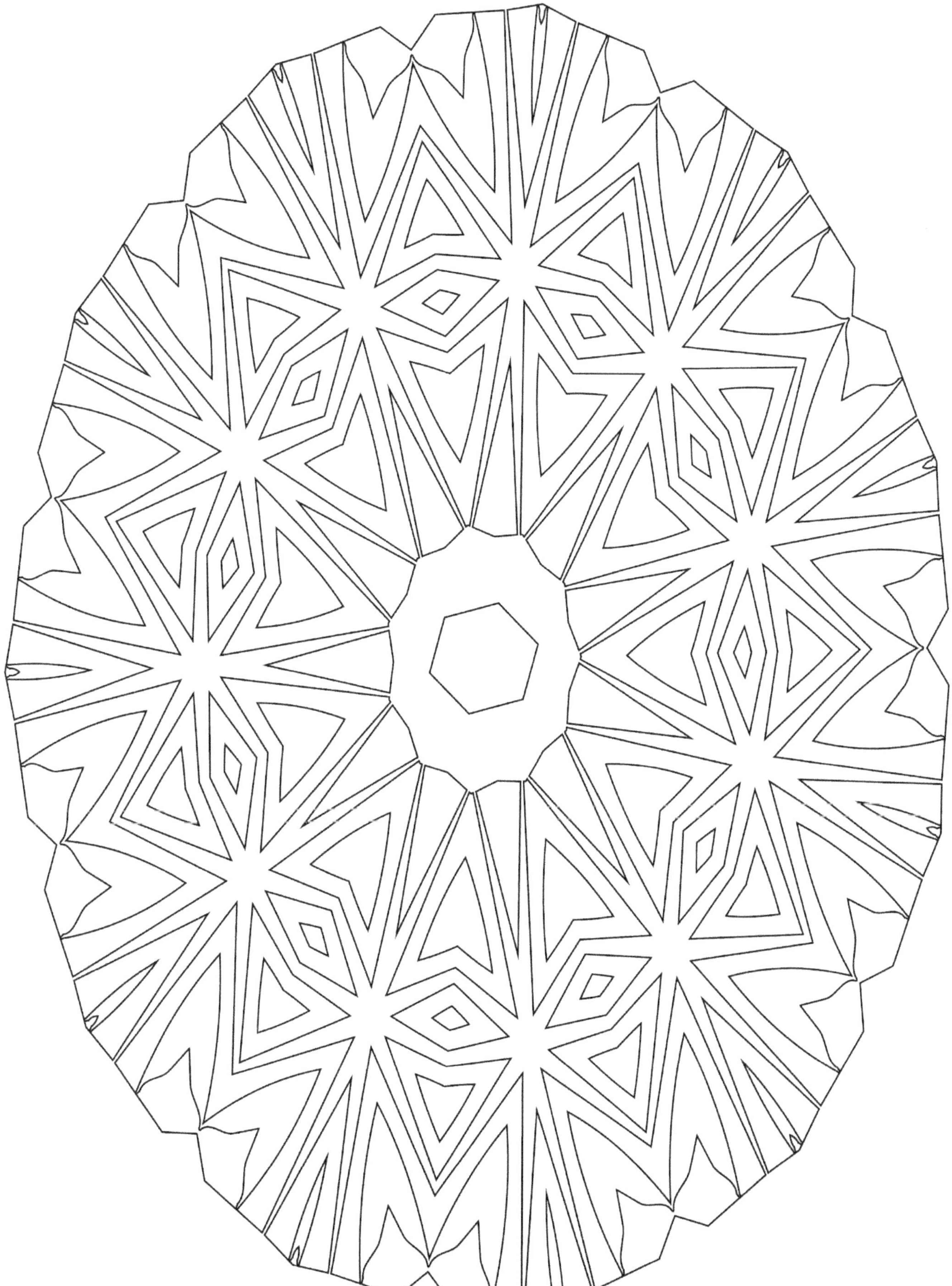

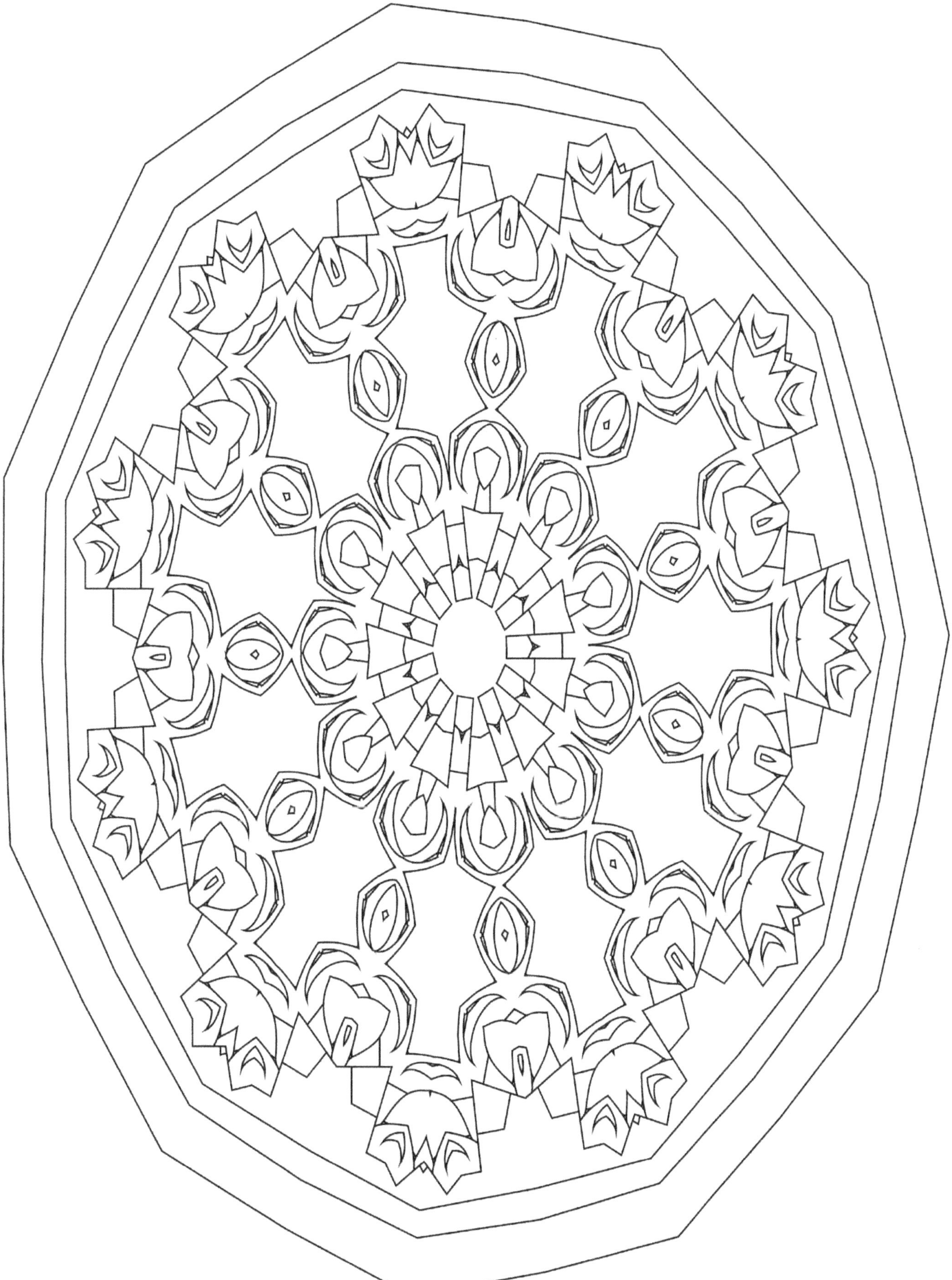

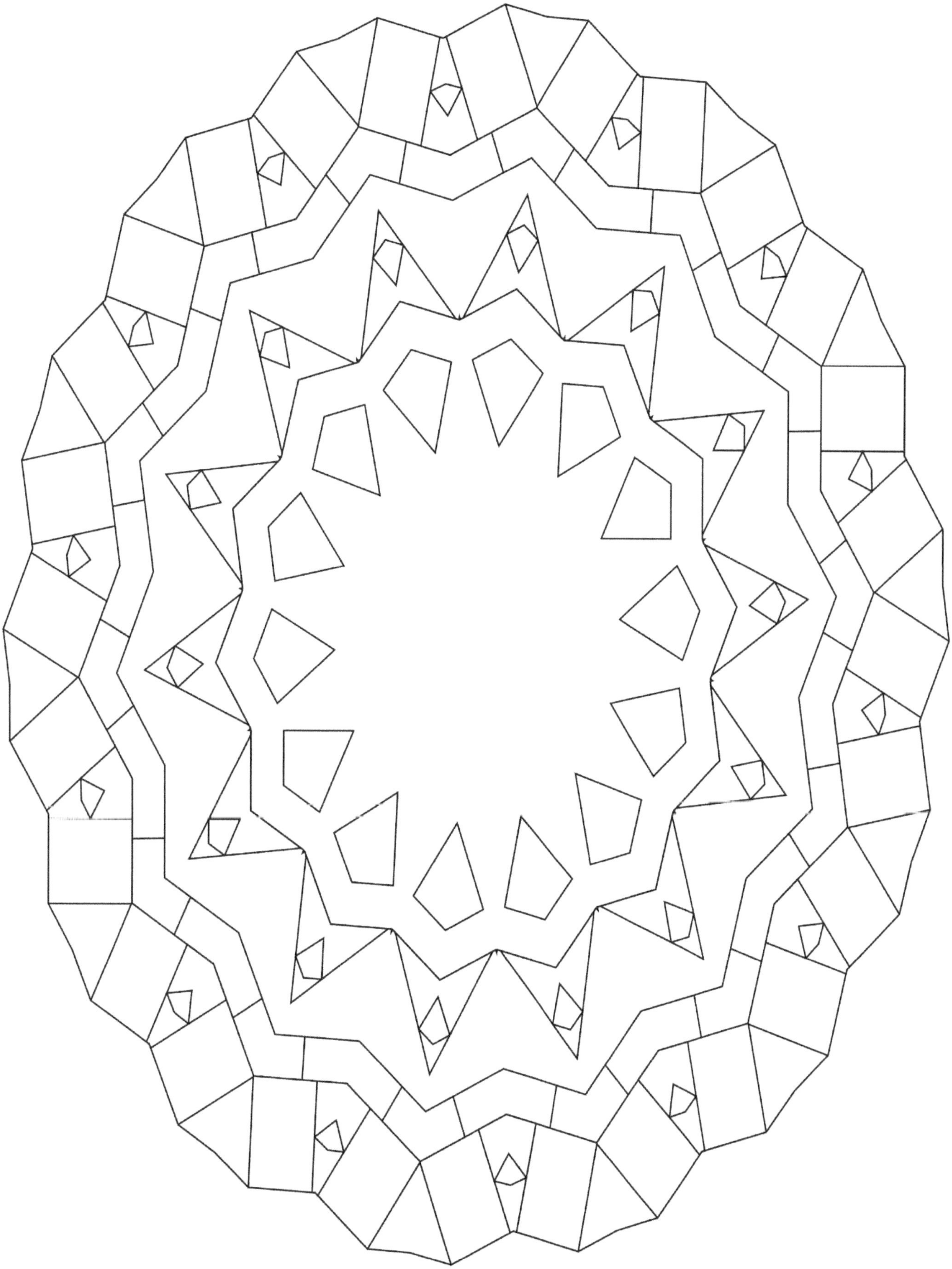

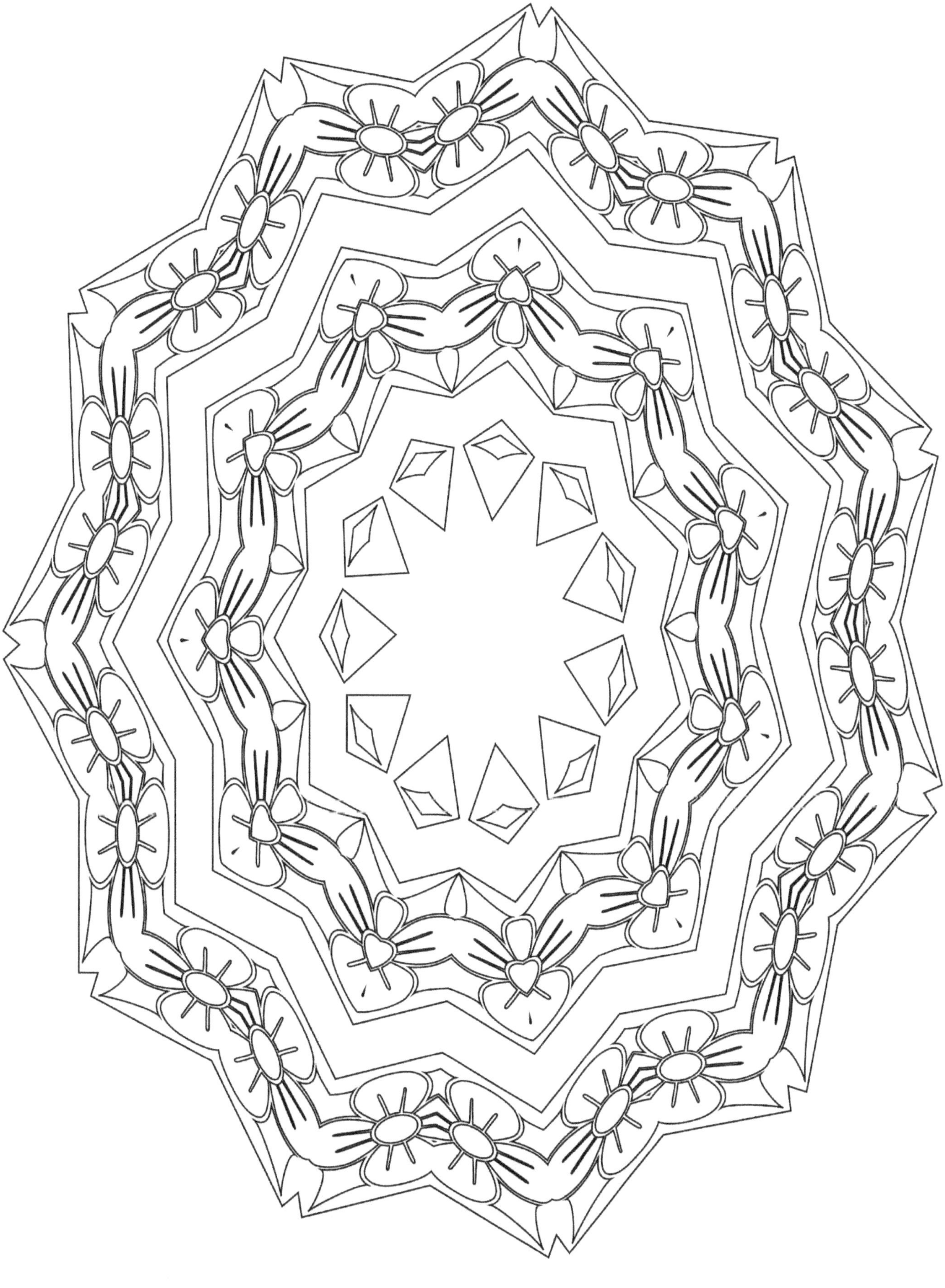

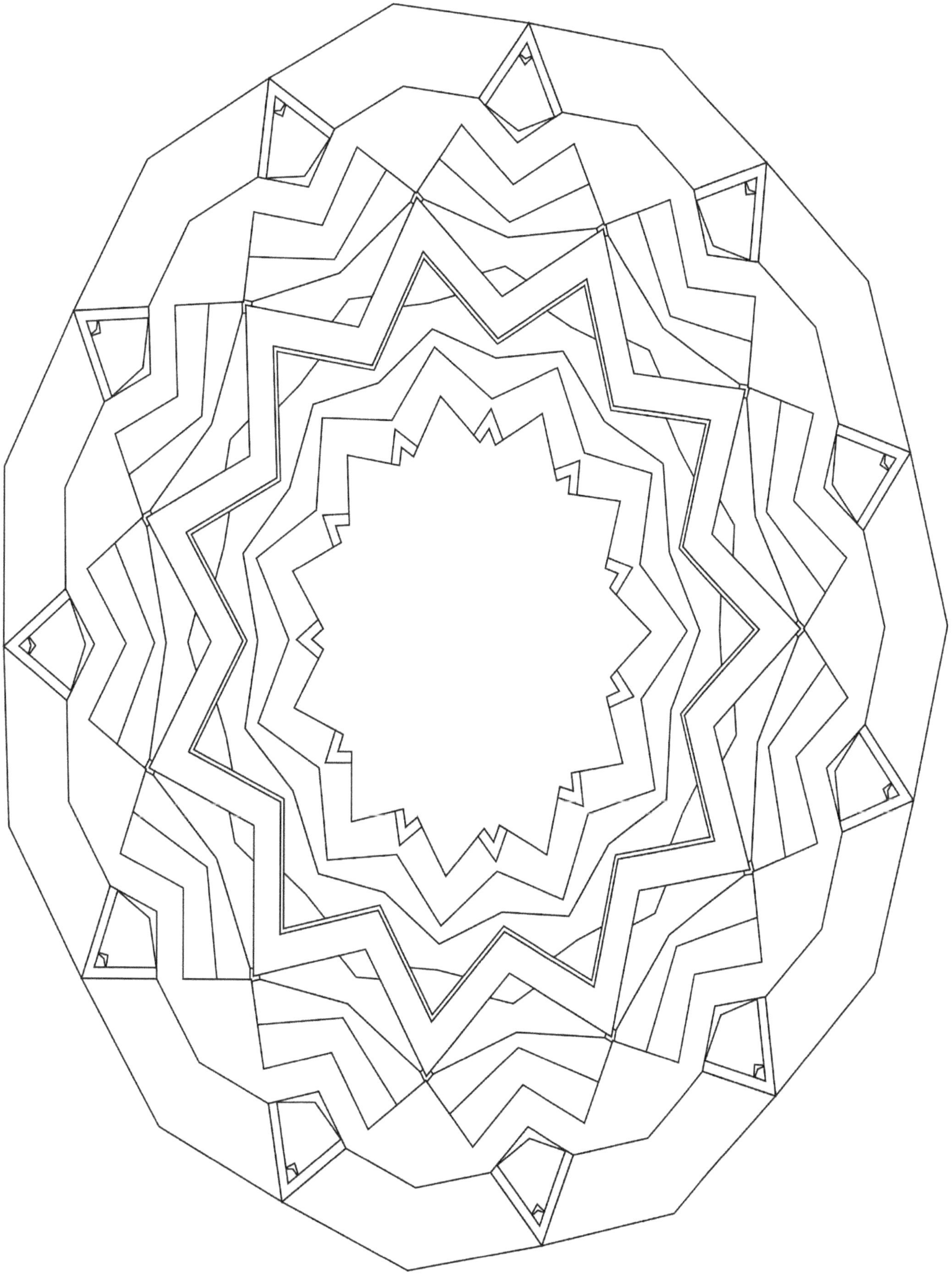

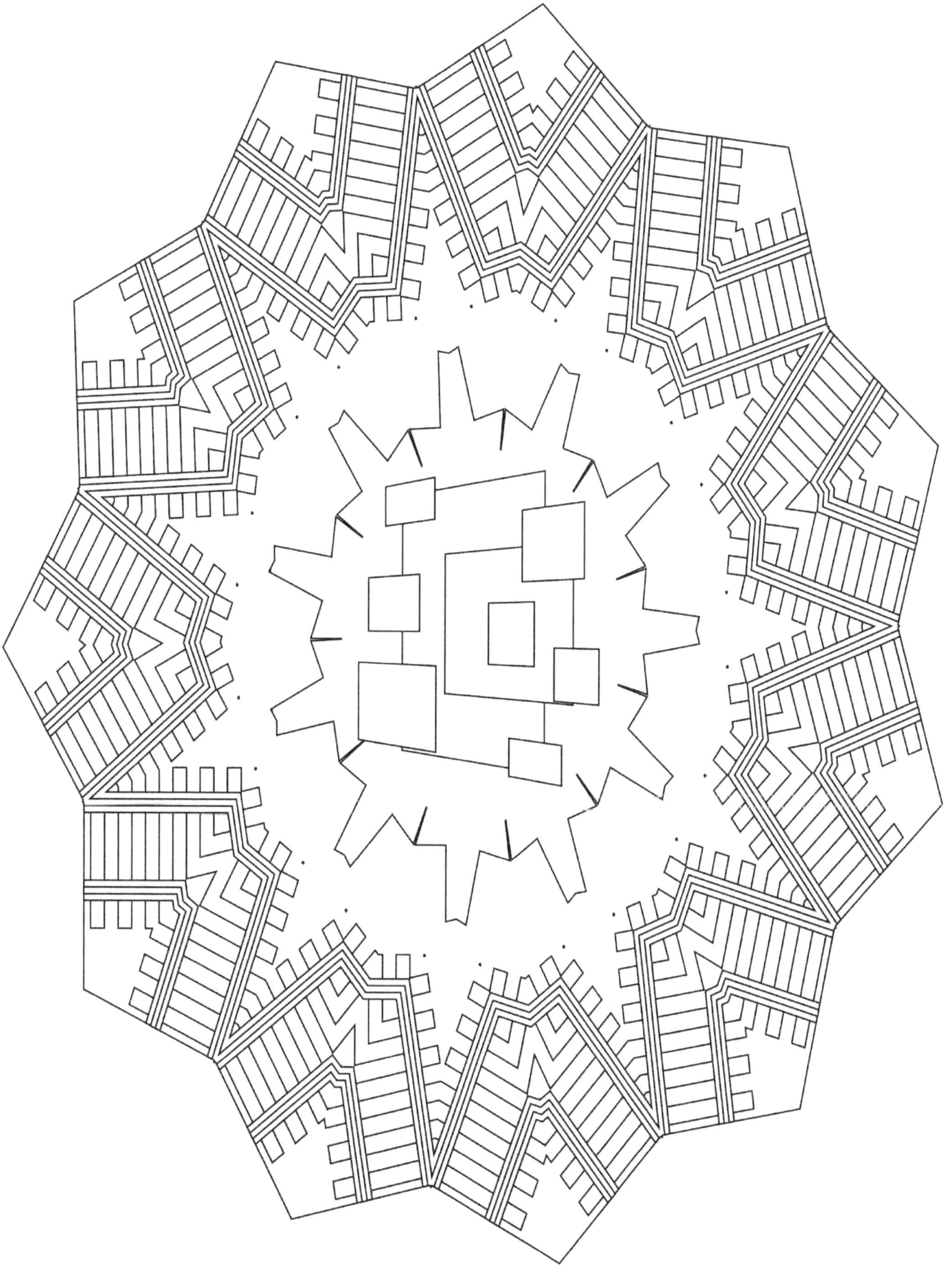

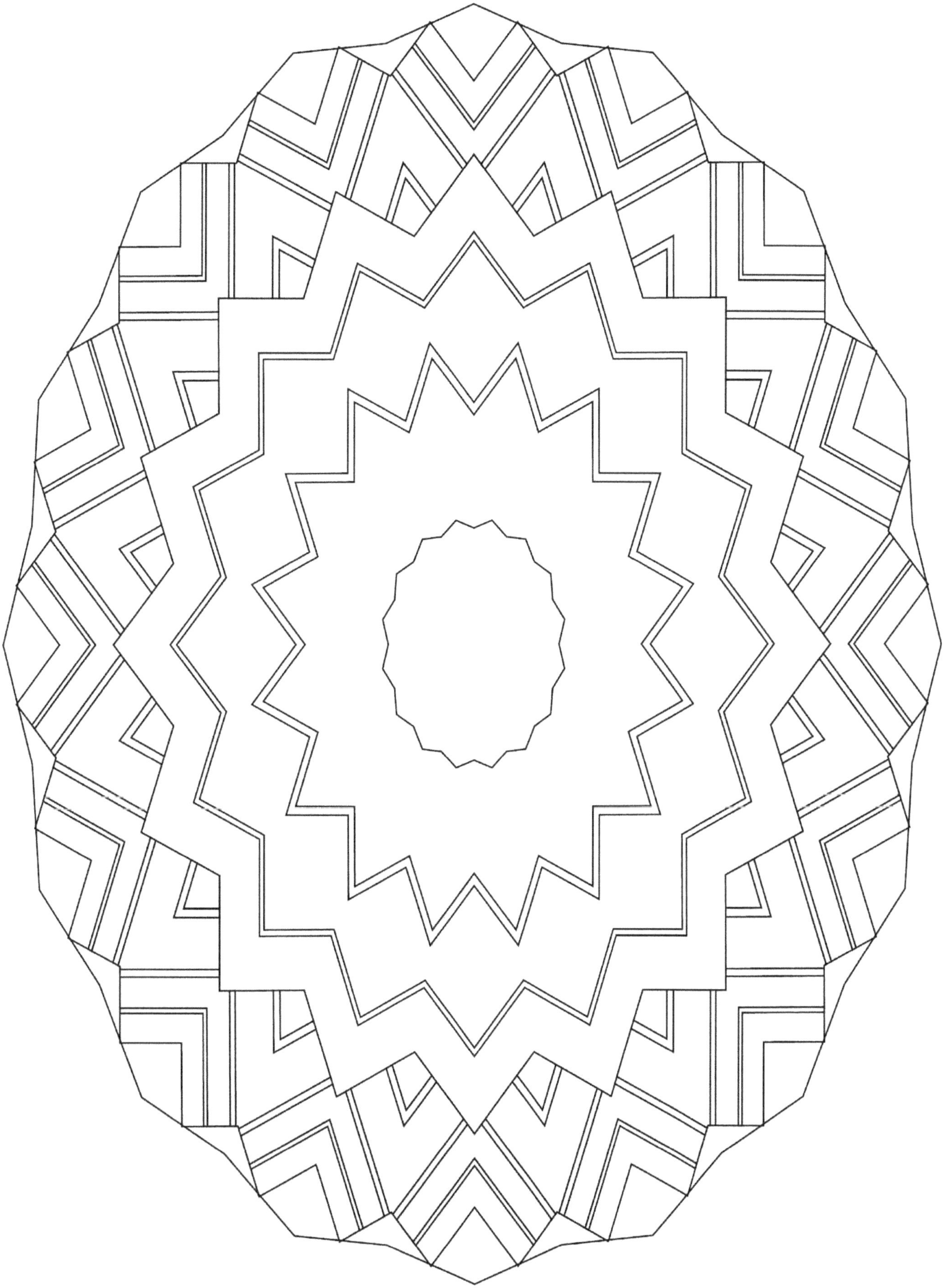

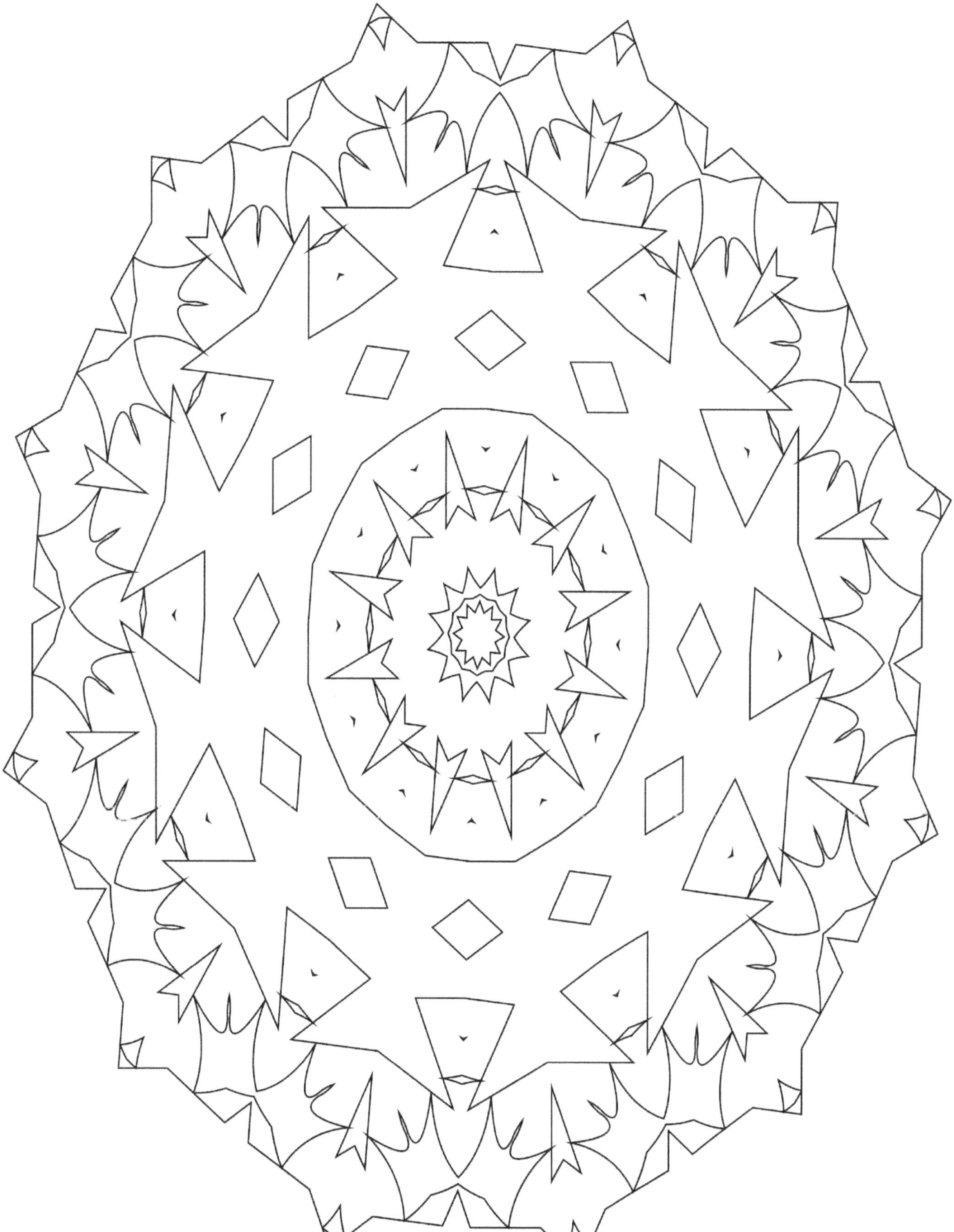

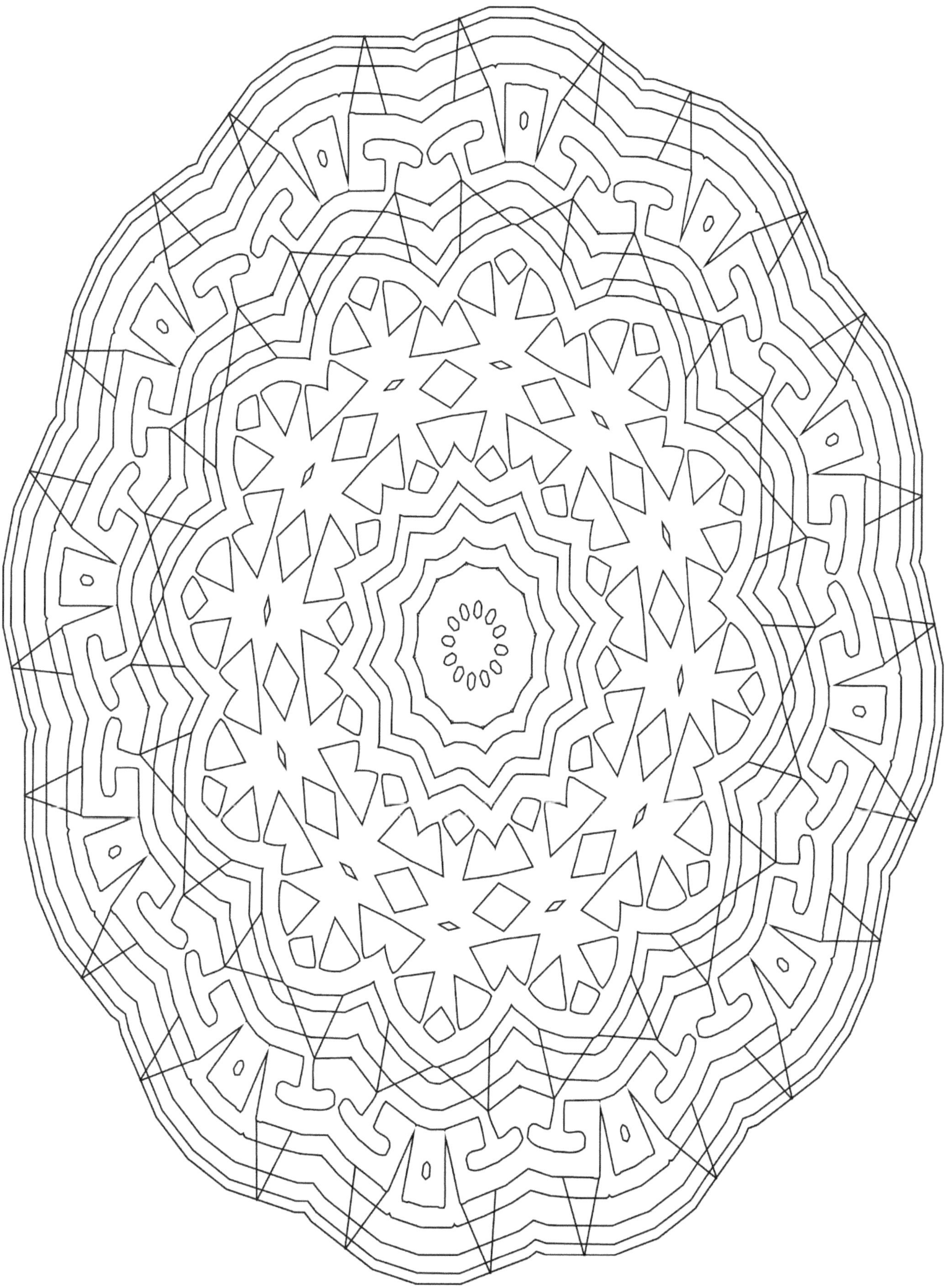

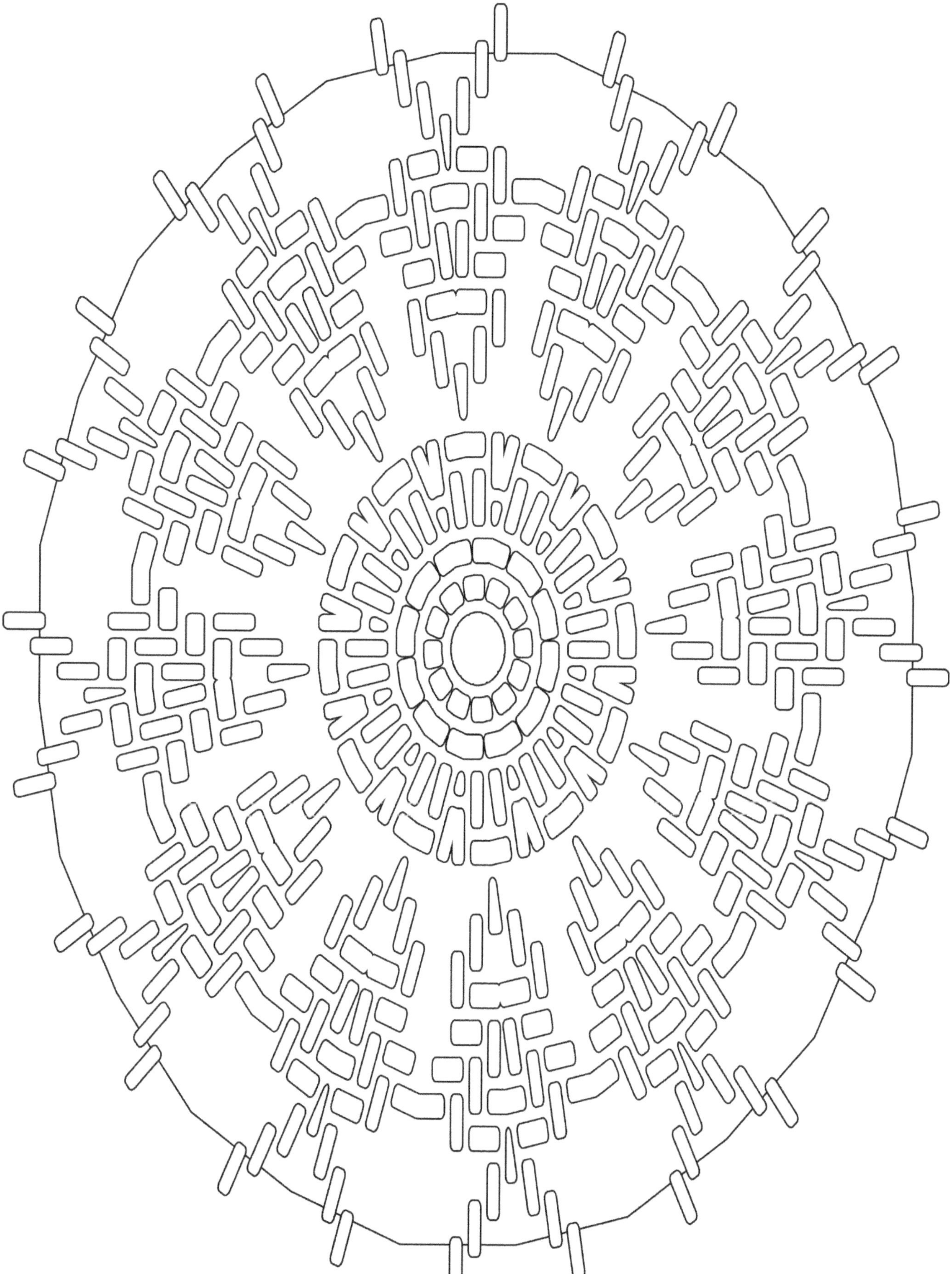

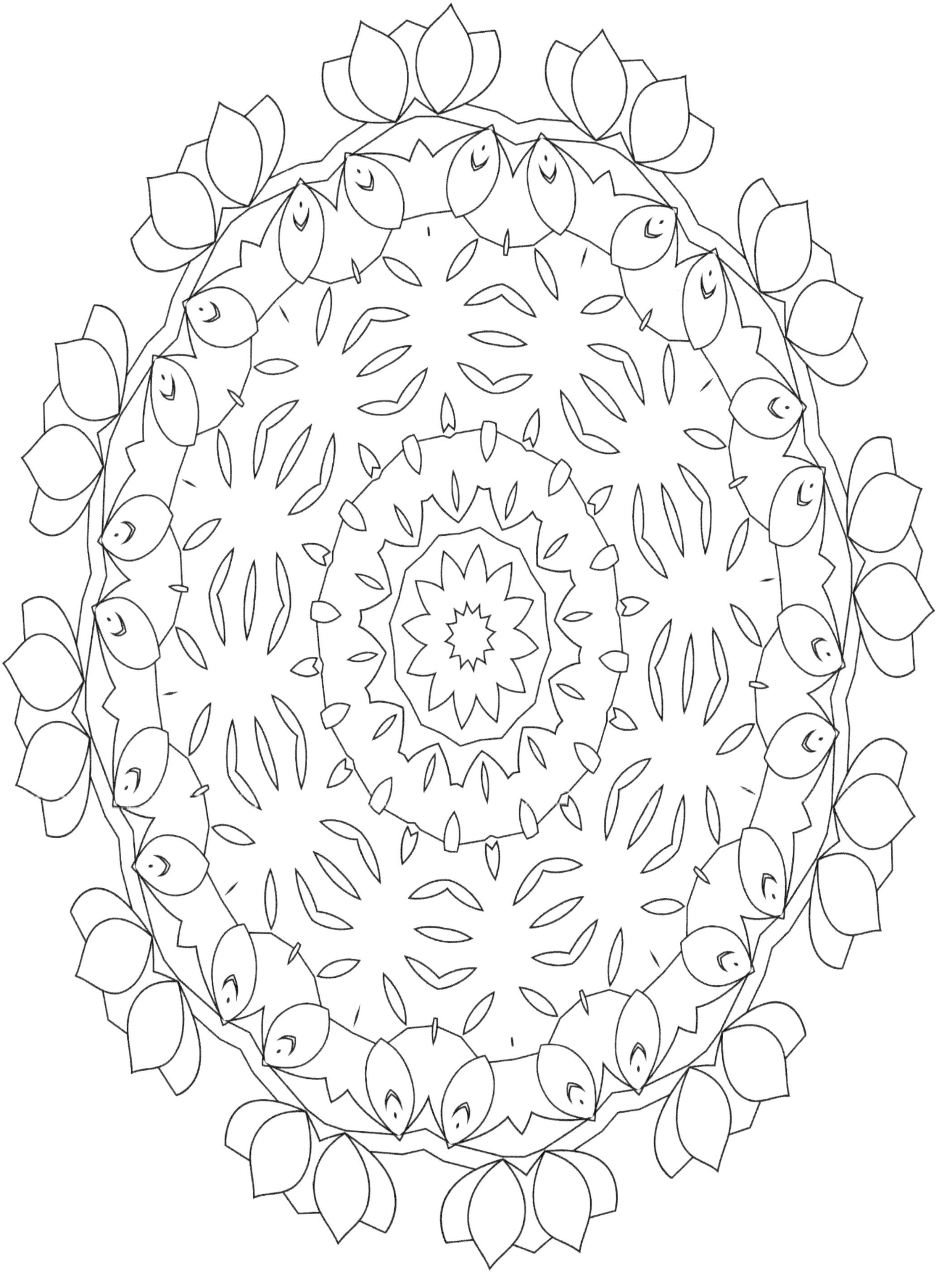

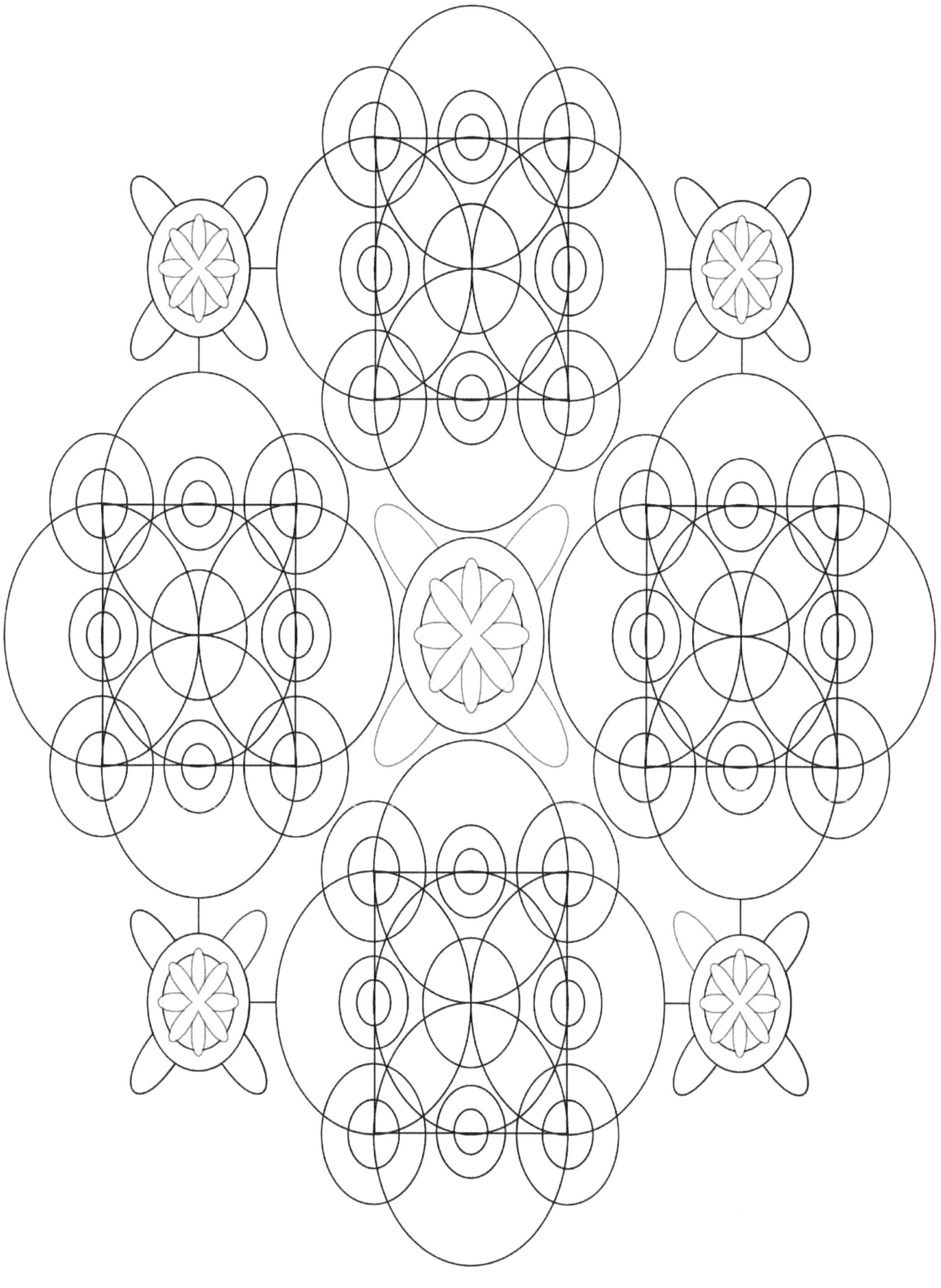

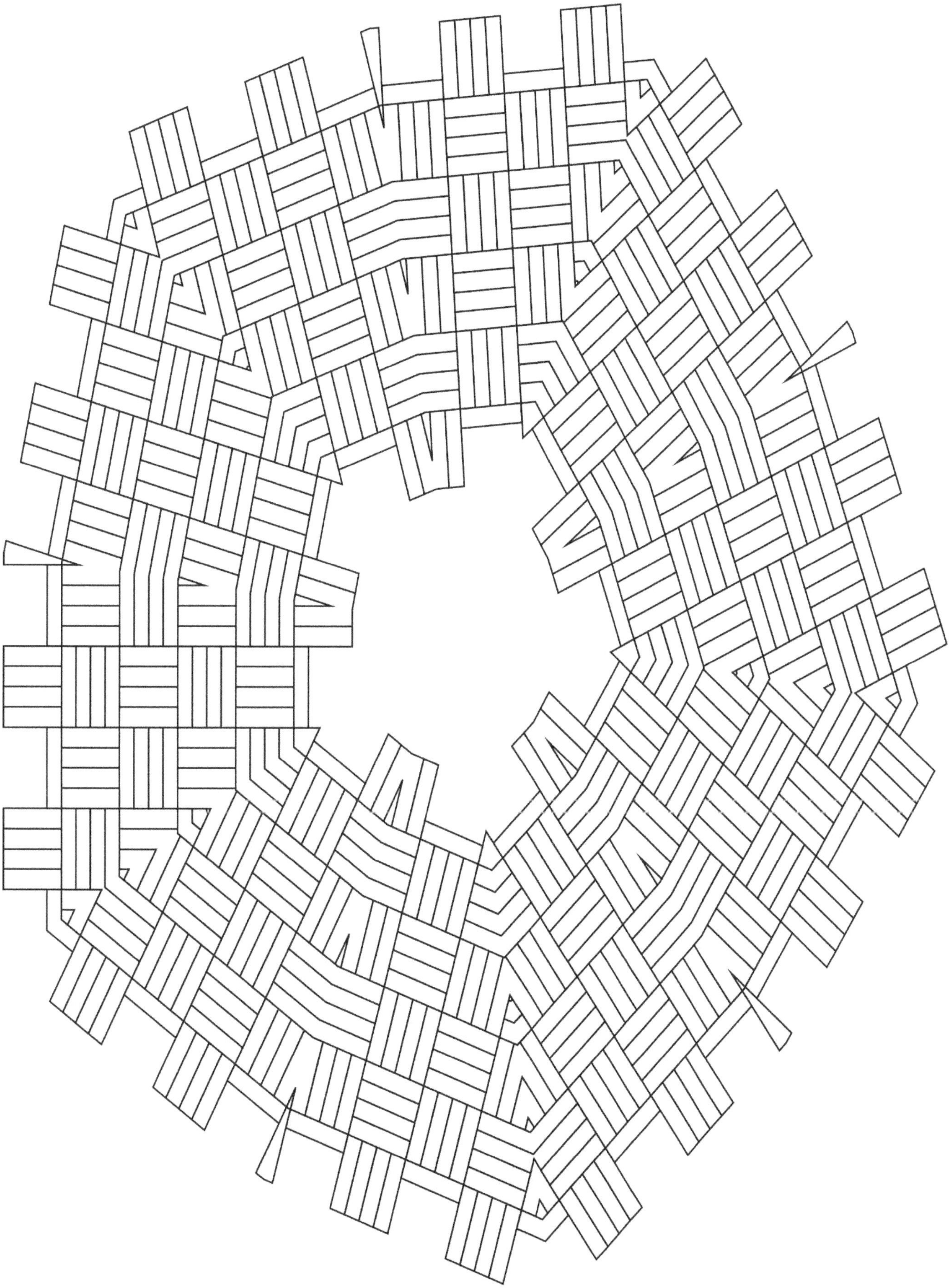

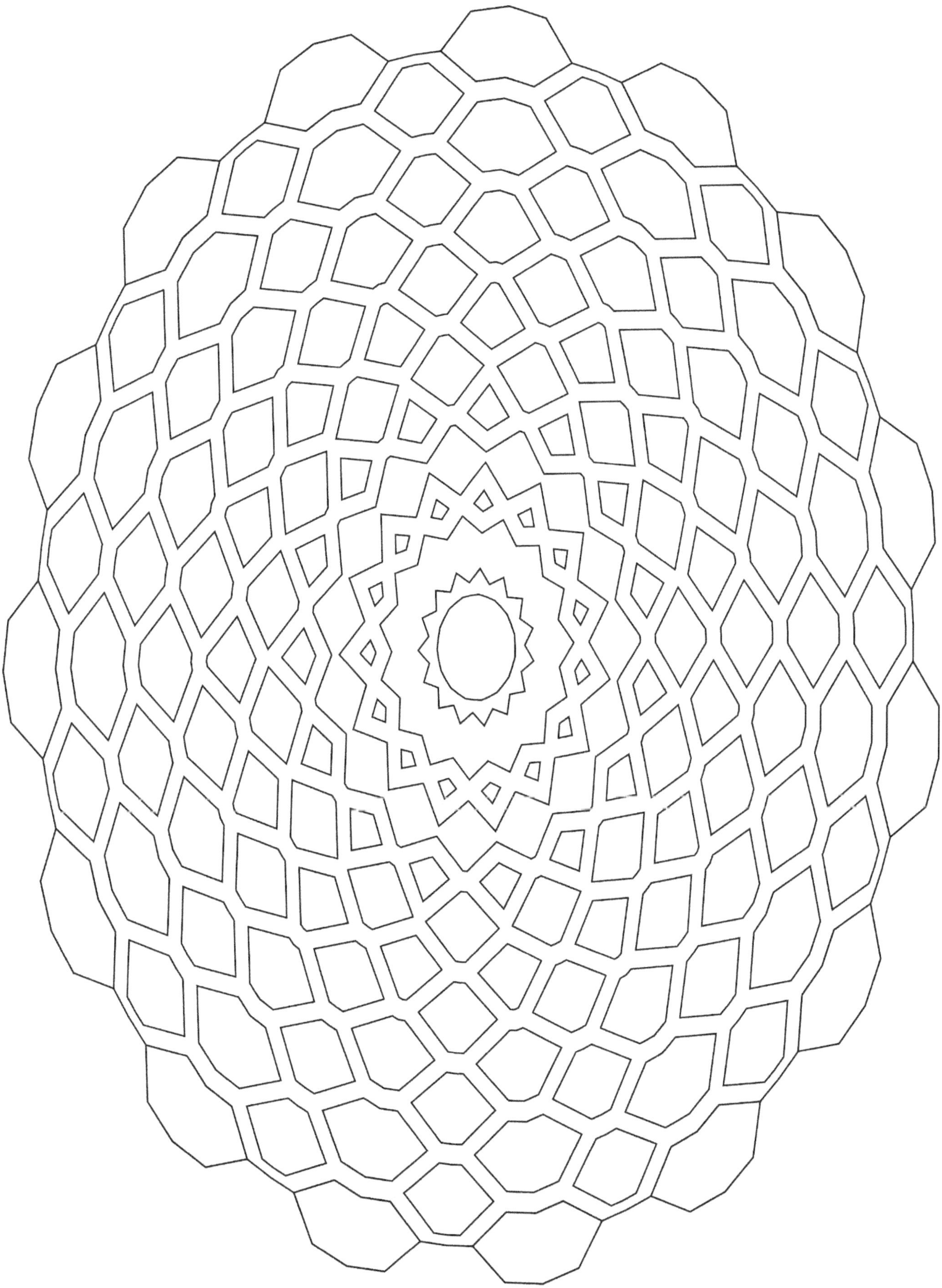

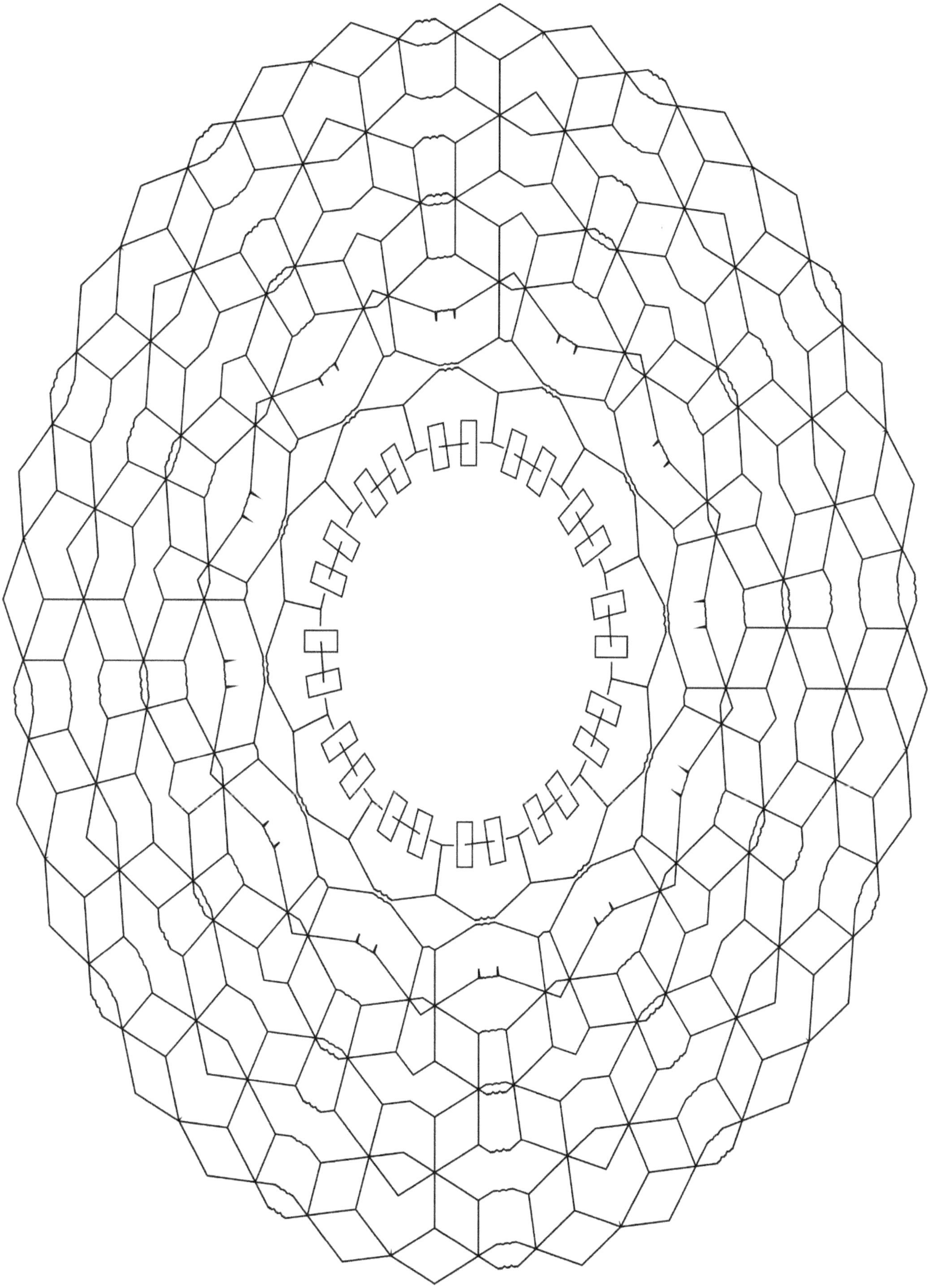

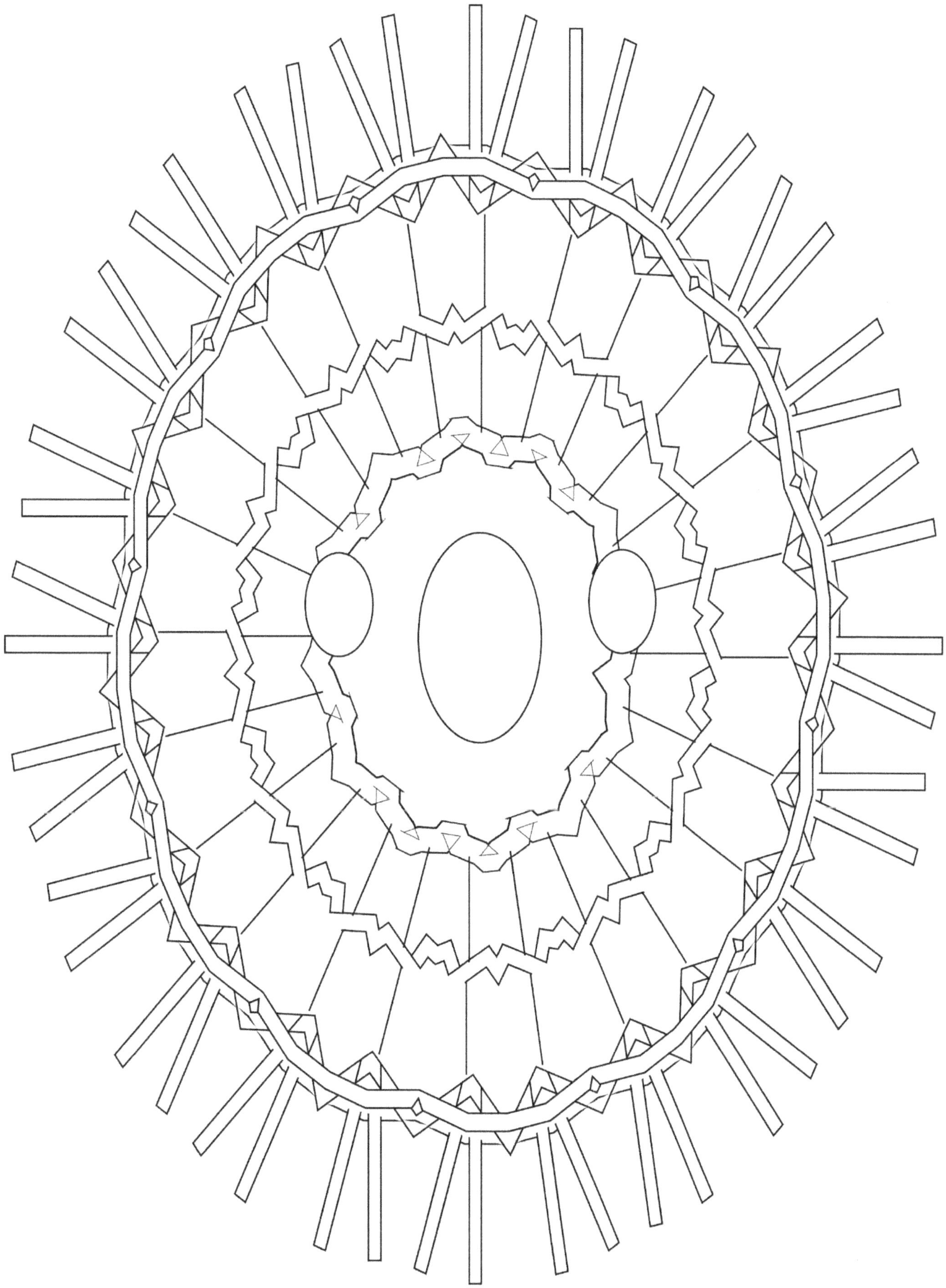

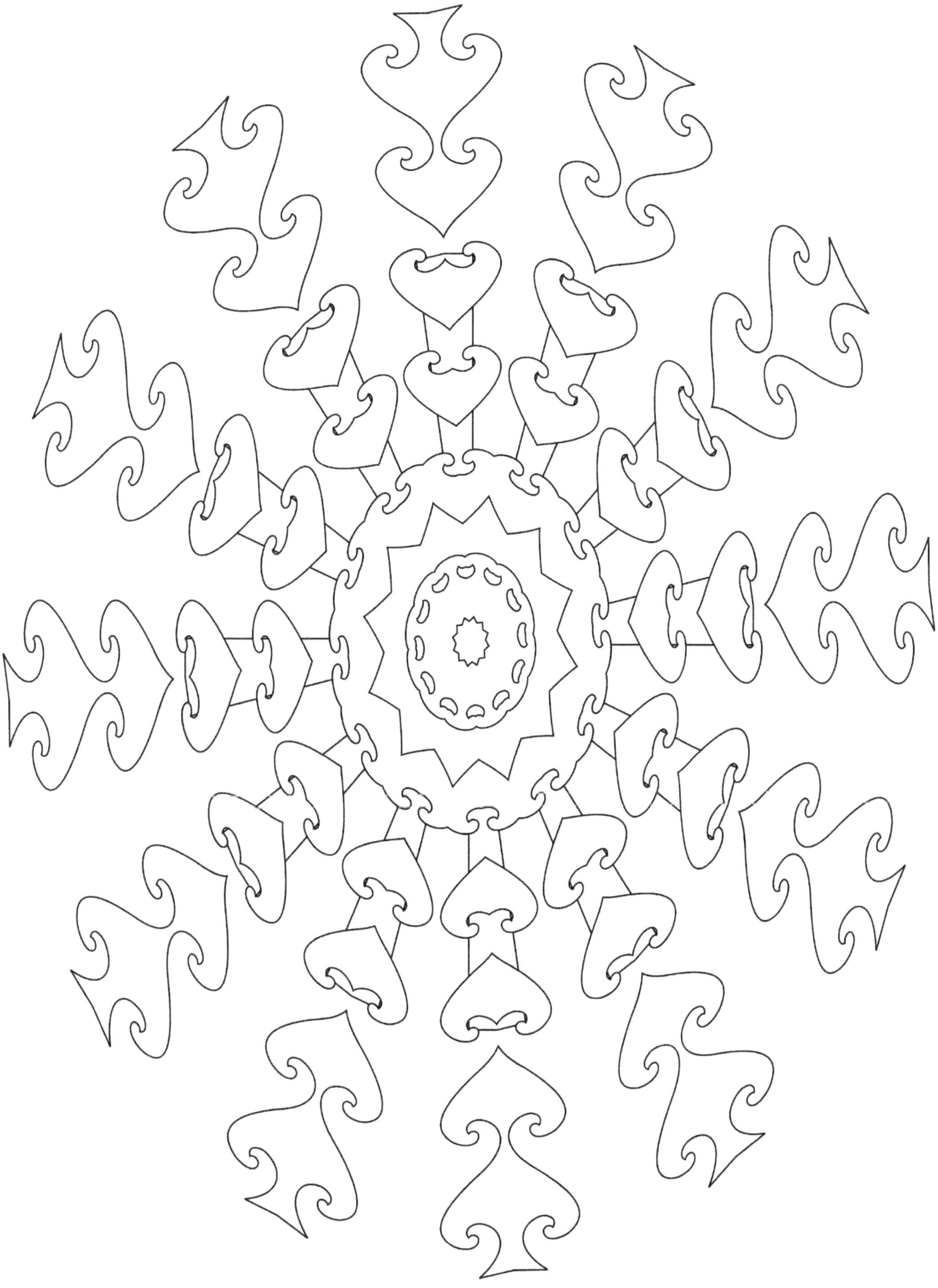

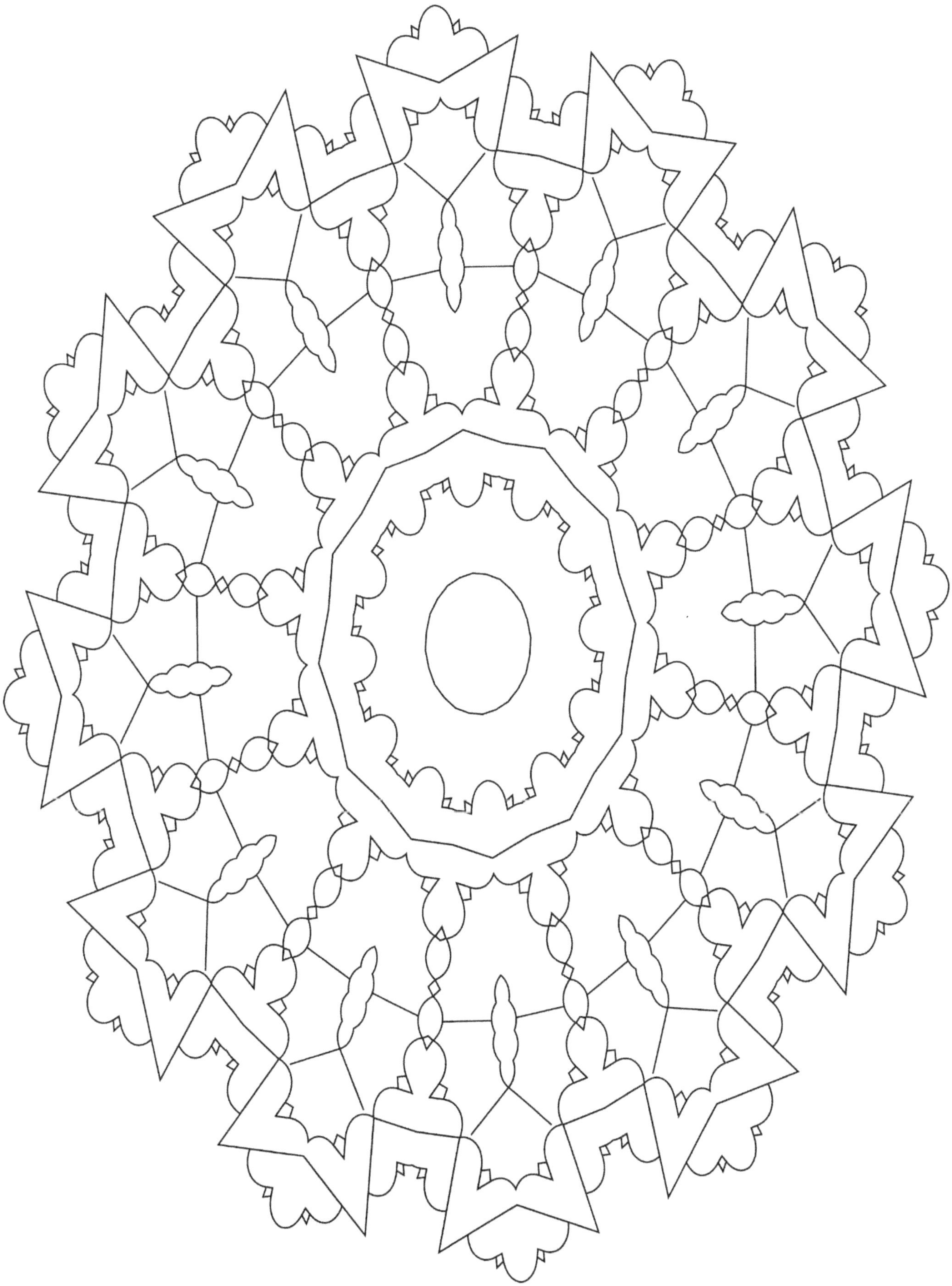

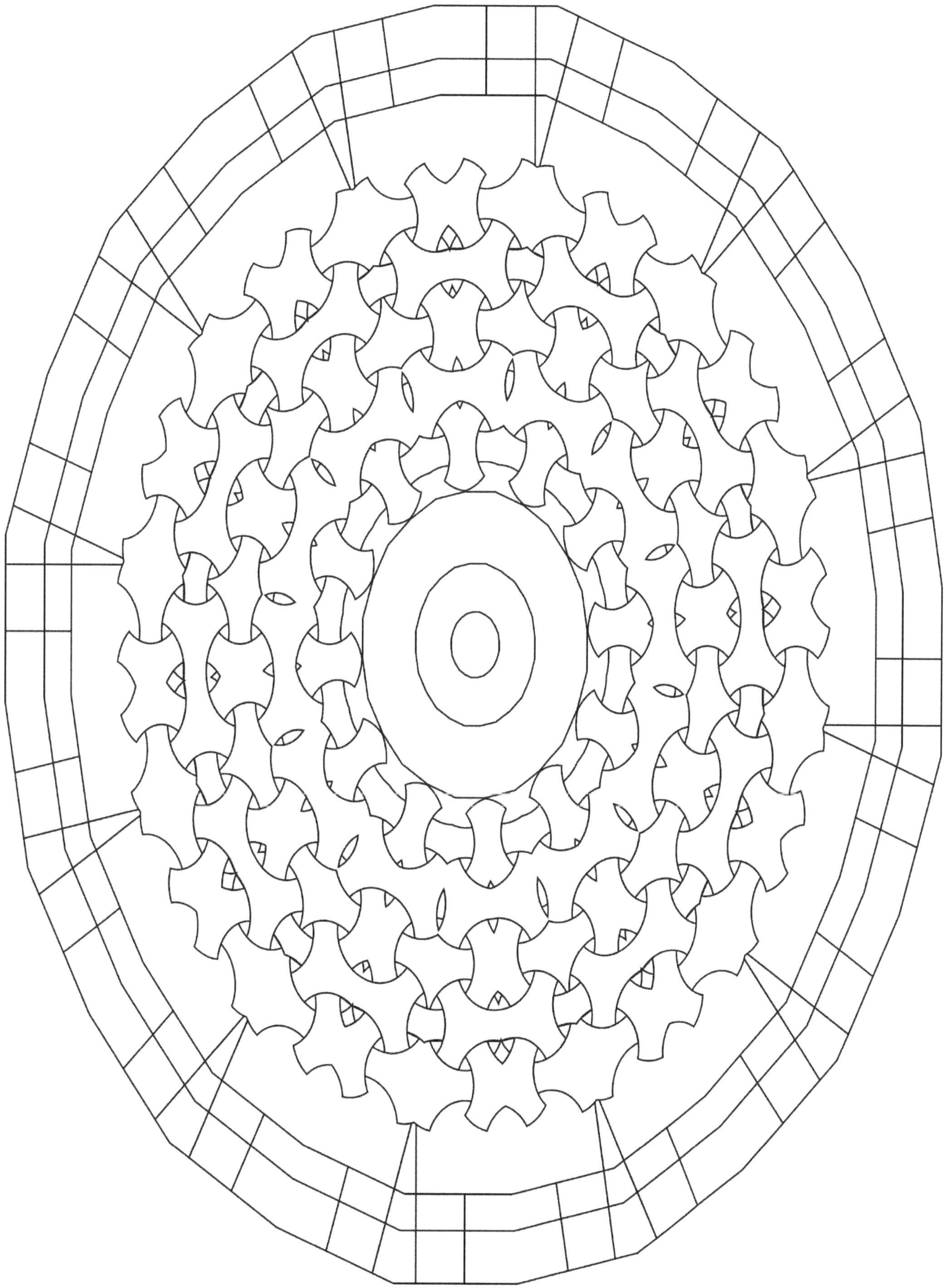

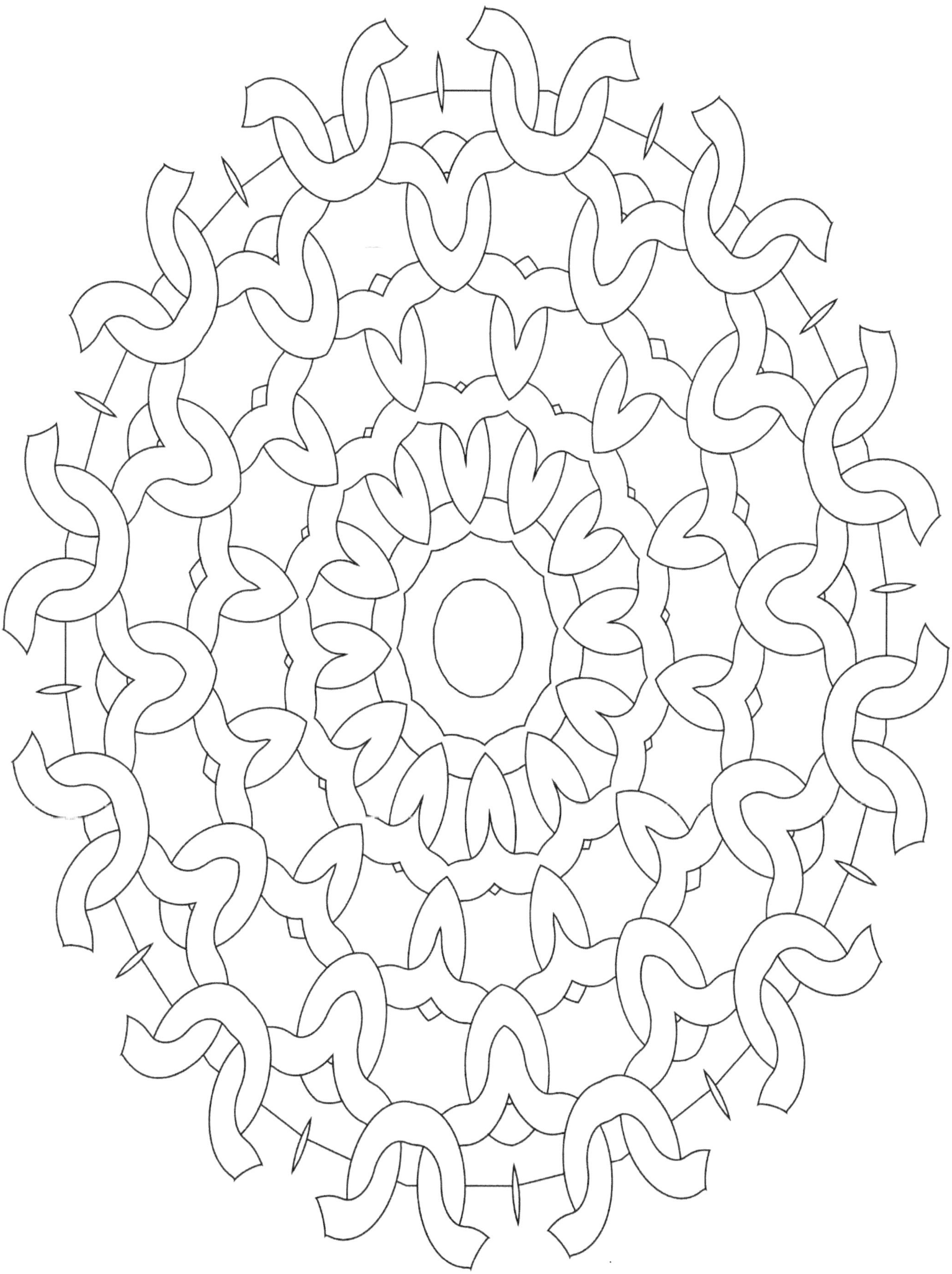

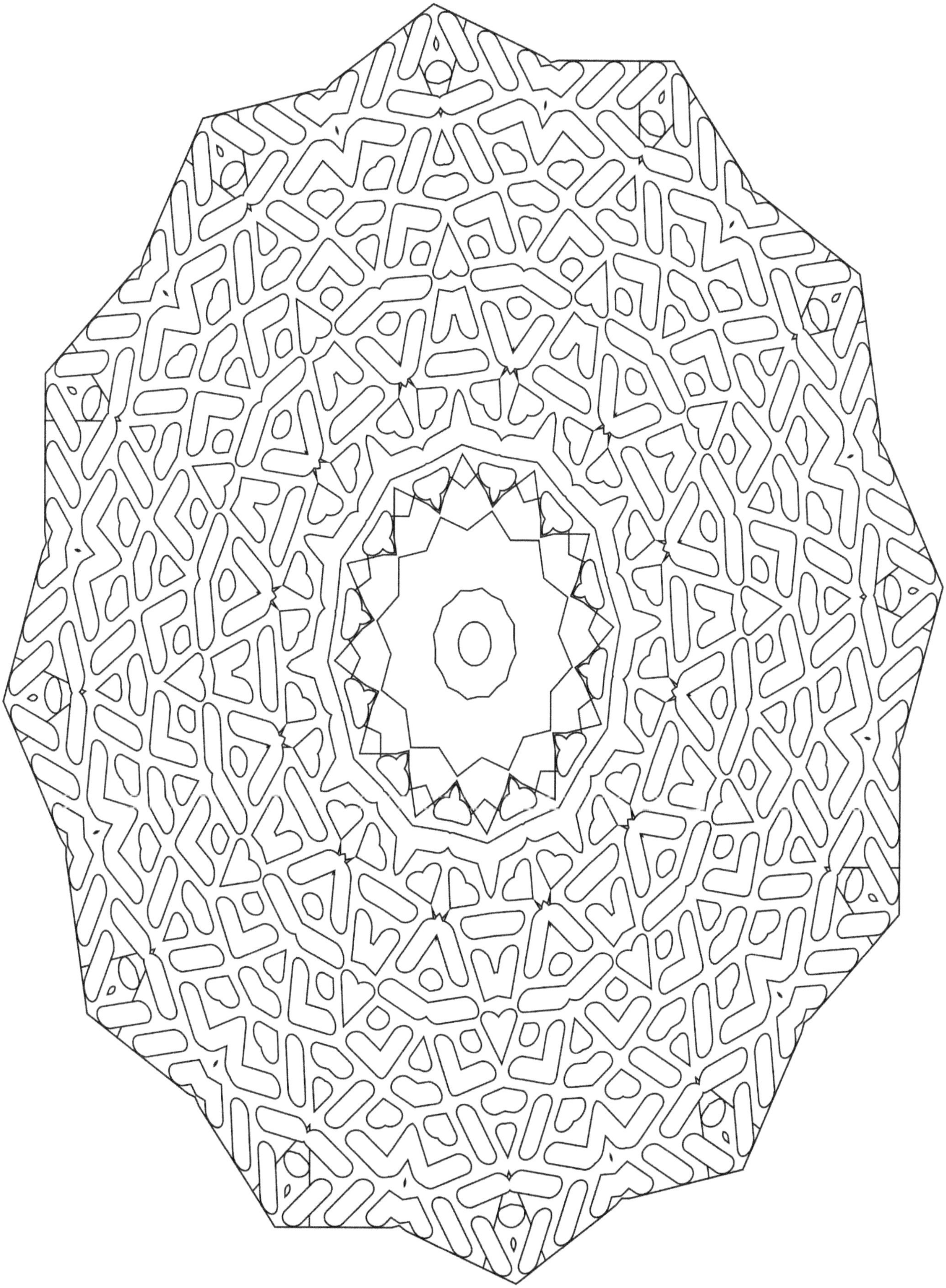

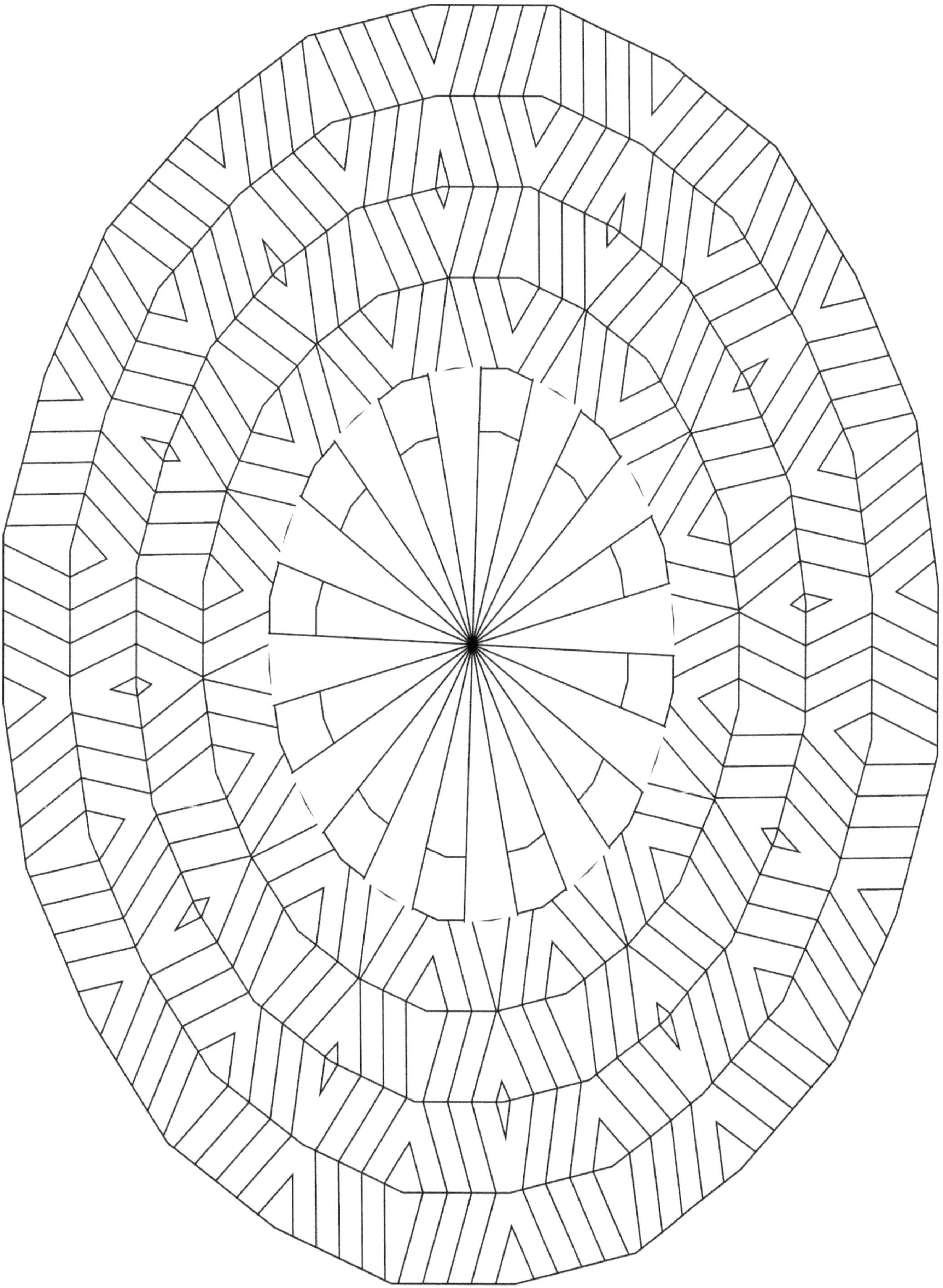

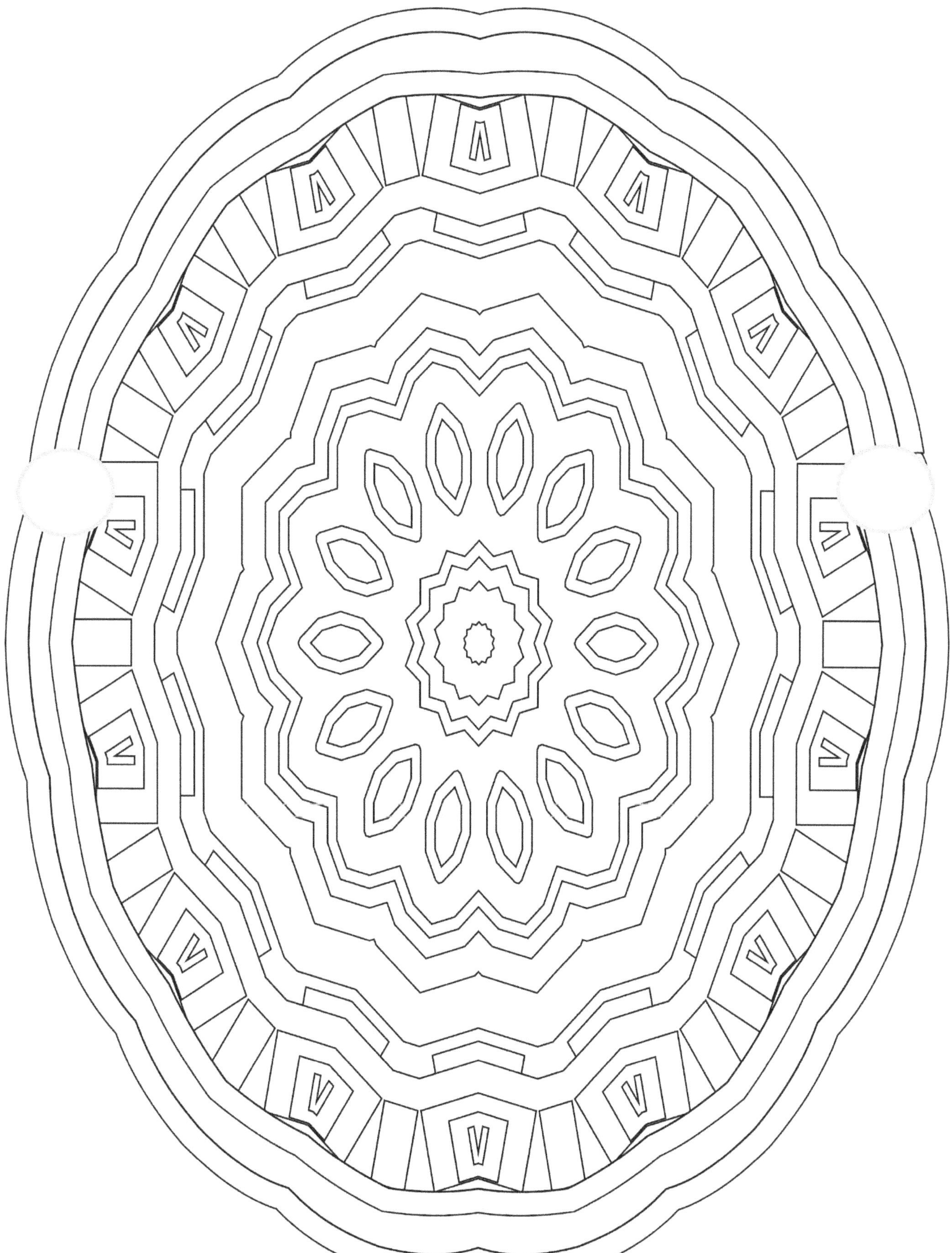

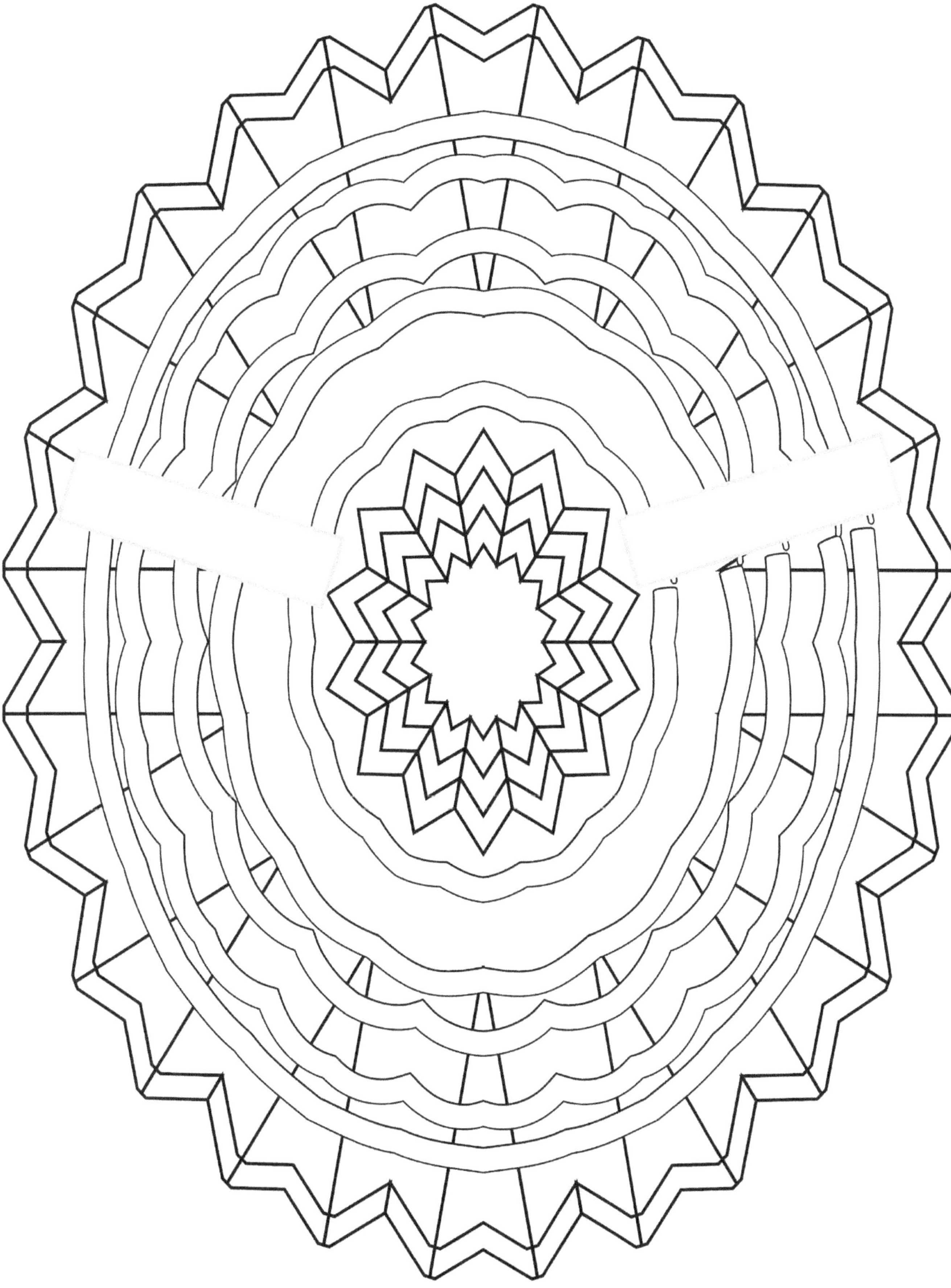

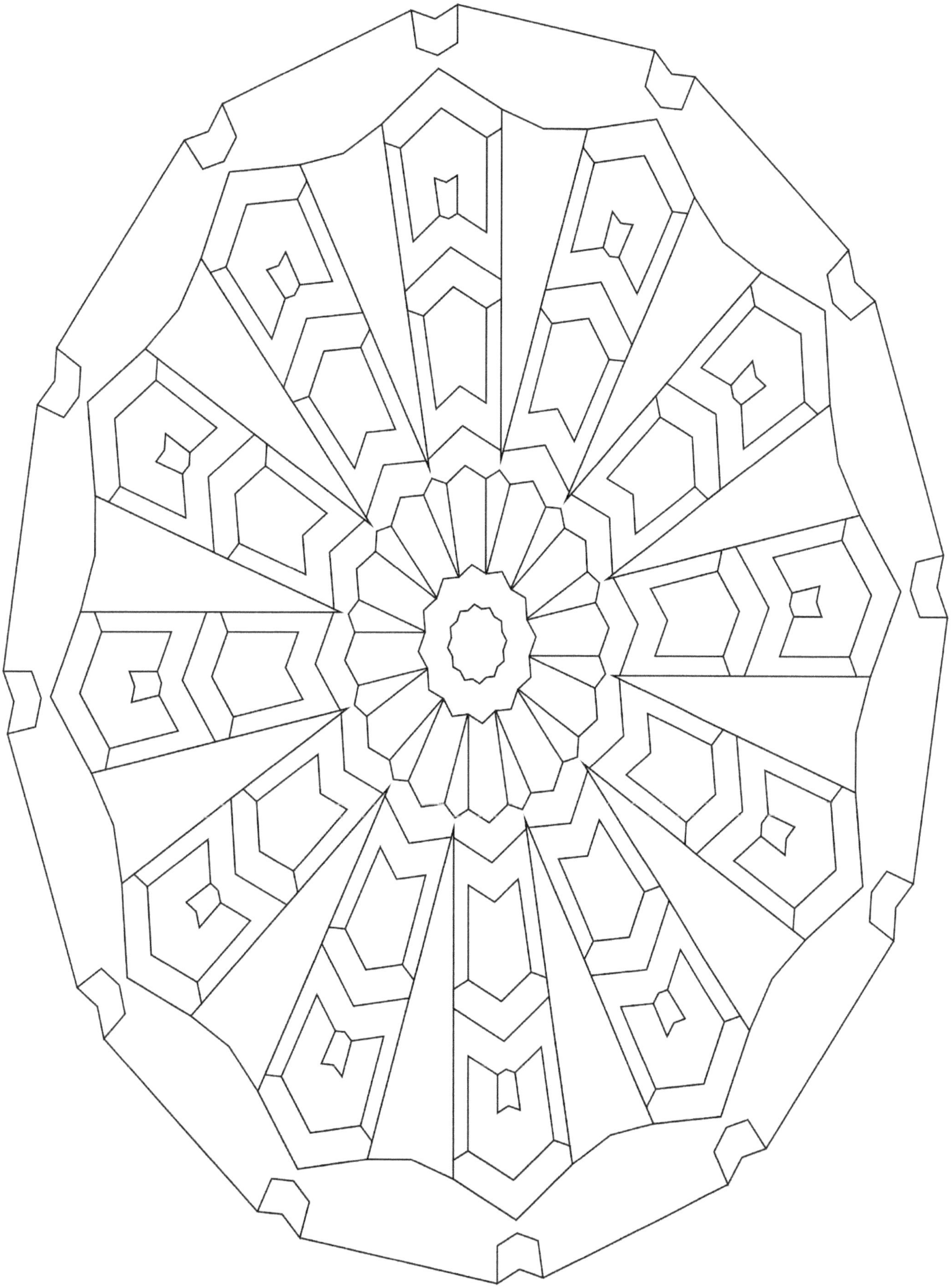

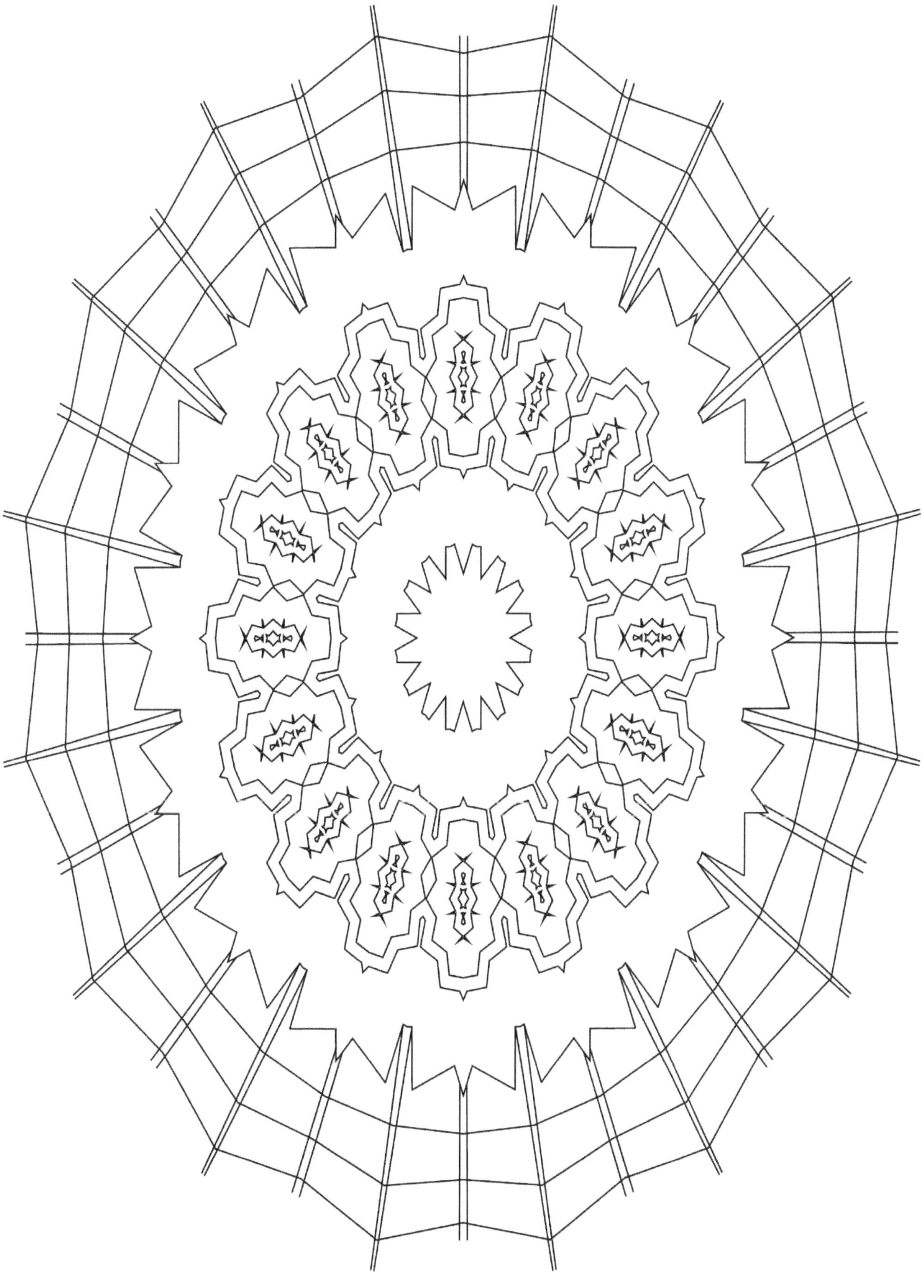

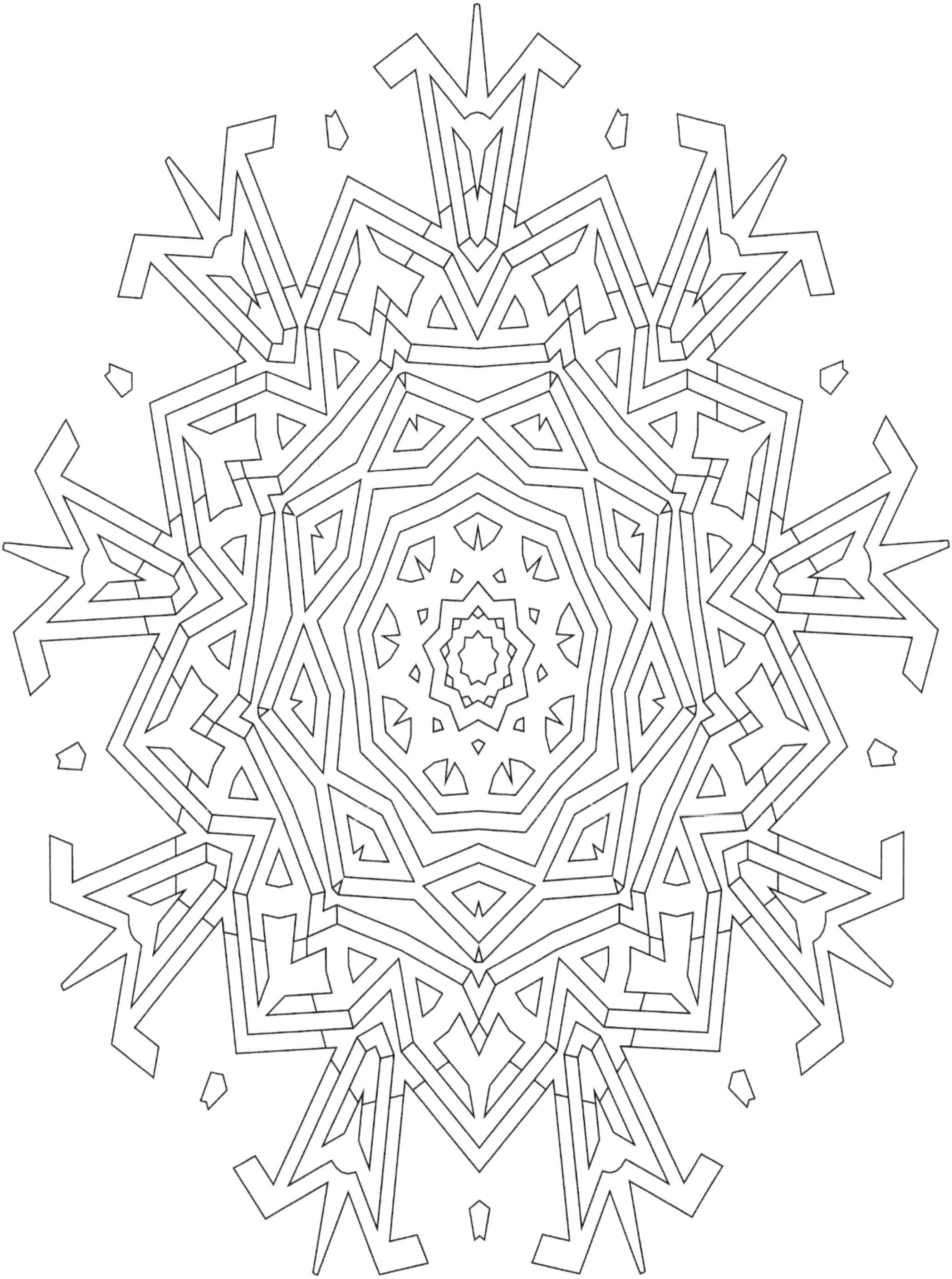

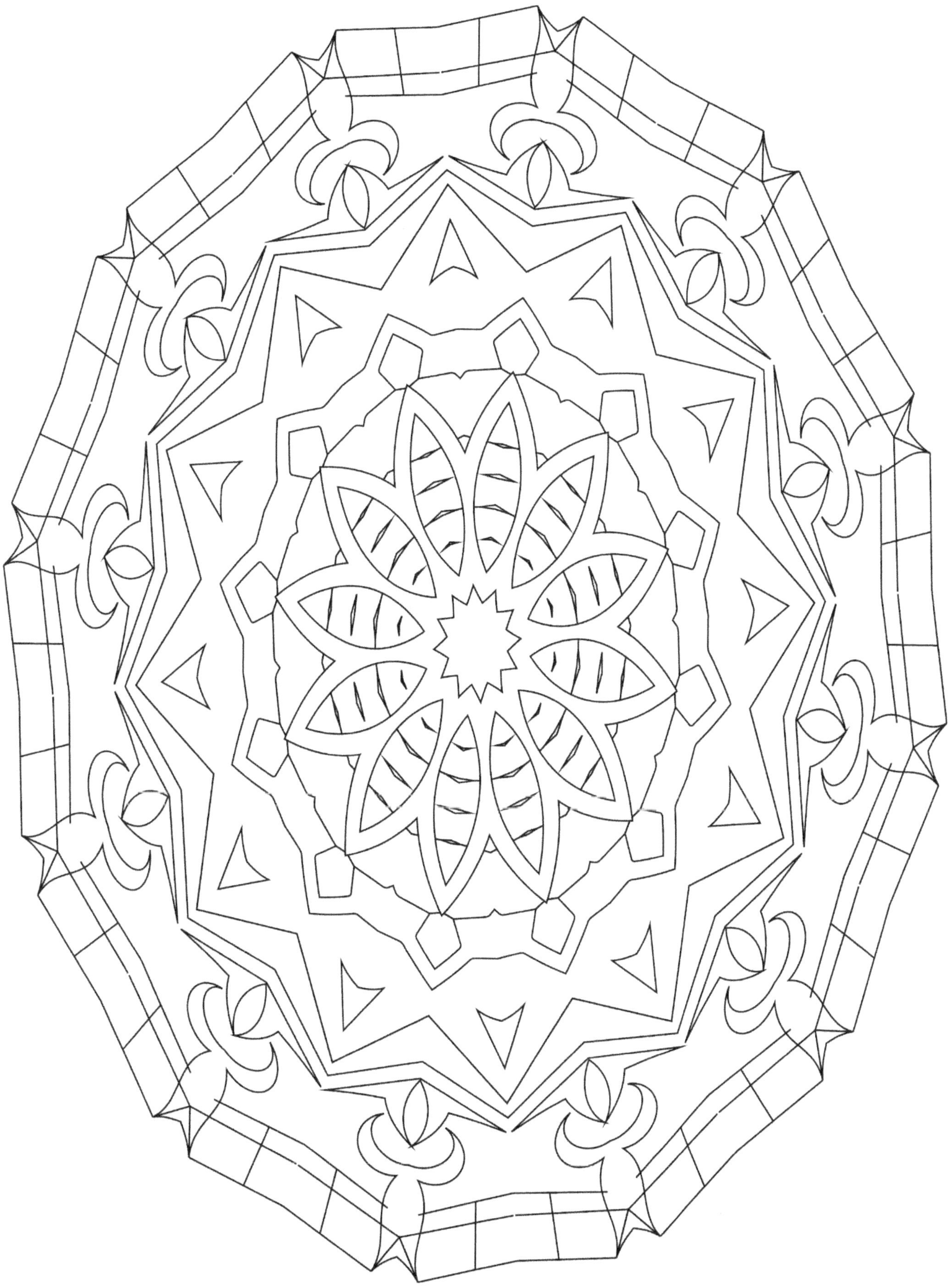

www.ingramcontent.com/pod-product-compliance
Lightning Source LLC
Chambersburg PA
CBHW080834180526
45168CB00006B/2676
* 9 7 8 1 5 1 4 7 7 2 8 5 0 *